D0691170

MINDSETS
&MOVES

To John: I am grateful for your admiring lens.

MINDSETS & MOVES

STRATEGIES THAT HELP
READERS TAKE CHARGE

GRADES 1-8

GRAVITY GOLDBERG

WITHDRAWN

A SAGE Company

FOR INFORMATION:

Corwin
A SAGE Company
2455 Teller Road
Thousand Oaks, California 91320
(800) 233-9936
www.corwin.com

SAGE Publications Ltd.
1 Oliver's Yard
55 City Road
London EC1Y 1SP
United Kingdom

SAGE Publications India Pvt. Ltd.
B 1/I 1 Mohan Cooperative Industrial Area
Mathura Road, New Delhi 110 044
India

SAGE Publications Asia-Pacific Pte. Ltd.
3 Church Street
#10-04 Samsung Hub
Singapore 049483

Publisher: Lisa Luedeke
Editor: Wendy Murray
Editorial Development Manager: Julie Nemer
Assistant Editor: Emeli Warren
Production Editor: Melanie Birdsall
Copy Editor: Melinda Masson
Typesetter: C&M Digitals (P) Ltd.
Proofreader: Scott Oney
Indexer: Molly Hall
Cover Designer: Gail Buschman
Interior Designer: Rose Storey
Marketing Managers: Maura Sullivan
                          and Rebecca Eaton

Copyright © 2016 by Corwin

All rights reserved. When forms and sample documents are included, their use is authorized only by educators, local school sites, and/or noncommercial or nonprofit entities that have purchased the book. Except for that usage, no part of this book may be reproduced or utilized in any form or by any means, electronic or mechanical, including photocopying, recording, or by any information storage and retrieval system, without permission in writing from the publisher.

All trademarks depicted within this book, including trademarks appearing as part of a screenshot, figure, or other image, are included solely for the purpose of illustration and are the property of their respective holders. The use of the trademarks in no way indicates any relationship with, or endorsement by, the holders of said trademarks.

Printed in the United States of America

ISBN 978-1-5063-1493-8

This book is printed on acid-free paper.

Certified Chain of Custody
Promoting Sustainable Forestry
www.sfiprogram.org
SFI-01268
SFI label applies to text stock

15 16 17 18 19 10 9 8 7 6 5 4 3 2 1

DISCLAIMER: This book may direct you to access third-party content via Web links, QR codes, or other scannable technologies, which are provided for your reference by the author(s). Corwin makes no guarantee that such third-party content will be available for your use and encourages you to review the terms and conditions of such third-party content. Corwin takes no responsibility and assumes no liability for your use of any third-party content, nor does Corwin approve, sponsor, endorse, verify, or certify such third-party content.

Contents

Acknowledgments   x

CHAPTER ONE

Reading on One's Own: What We Really Mean by Take-Charge Independence   1

What Does It Really Mean to Read on One's Own?   4
- Parts of a Reading Workshop   4

Examining Teacher Roles   8

Taking the Spotlight Off the Teacher   11

The Facets of Ownership   14

How Rigor Fits In   17

The Pitfalls of Turning Play Into Work: Motivation Challenges   18

What's Next?   21

CHAPTER TWO

Shifting Roles: Be a Miner, a Mirror, a Model, a Mentor   23

The Gift of Problems: Creating a Willingness to Struggle   23

Shifting Roles Toward Reader Ownership   26

What Shifted?   29

Taking on New Teacher Roles: The 4 *Ms*   31

How Ownership Sits Within the Gradual Release Model   32

What's Next?   37

CHAPTER THREE

Being an Admirer: Looking at Readers With Curiosity   39

Admiring Allows Us to See What Is There   40

Admiring Gives Us Glimpses Into Our Students' Minds   43

Admiring Lets Us See Potential   45

Admiring Helps Us Recognize Individuality   47

Admiring Pushes Us to Be Precise   48

Admiring Gives Us the Small and Big Picture   50

Admiring Supports a Growth Mindset   52

Admiring Creates Growth Mindset Expectations   54

Andrew Levine Photography

Language Impacts Mindset   55
Admiring Impacts Our Guiding Questions   56
Start Admiring!   57

CHAPTER FOUR

Creating Space for Ownership: A Photo Tour of Reading Classrooms

Creating Space for Ownership:
A Photo Tour of Reading Classrooms   59
Reading Process Spiral   60
Reading Workshop Space   62
Class Meeting Area   63
Reading Notebooks   65
Tracking Reading Volume   70
Class Goals Chart   71
Book Club Tools and Spaces   73
Student Intentions   74
Small Group Instruction   75
Reading Nooks   76
Student Reflections   82
Conclusion   89

Andrew Levine Photography

CHAPTER FIVE

Andrew Levine Photography

Be a Miner: Uncovering
Students' Reading Processes   91
Using a Five-Step Process   92
• Step 1: Set a Purpose   93
• Step 2: Observe the Reader   94
• Step 3: Ask Process-Oriented Questions   96
• Step 4: Listen   96
• Step 5: Collect   98
Uncovering One Student's Reading Process   100
Uncovering a Class's Reading Processes   107
Choosing When to Be a Miner   110
Admiring Trouble   111
• The "Trouble"   111
• Examining the "Trouble"
  With an Admiring Lens   111
• What I Did   112
• What I Learned   113
Conclusion   113

Andrew Levine Photography

CHAPTER SIX

Be a Mirror: Giving Feedback That Reinforces a Growth Mindset II7

Feedback Teaches 119
Preparing to Give Feedback 119
- Quality 1: Be Specific 120
- Quality 2: Name What Is 121
- Quality 3: Focus on the Process 122
- Quality 4: Make Sure It Can Transfer 124
- Quality 5: Take Yourself Out of It 125

Being a Mirror to a Small Group 126
Being a Mirror to the Whole Class 129
Admiring Trouble 130
- The "Trouble" 130
- Examining the "Trouble" With an Admiring Lens 130
- What I Did 131
- What I Learned 133

Conclusion 133

Andrew Levine Photography

CHAPTER SEVEN

Be a Model: Showing Readers What We Do 135

Being a Model 137
- Action 1: Set the Context by Explaining 137
- Action 2: Show the Steps by Demonstrating 137
- Action 3: Summarizing by Naming What Was Done 142

Being a Model to One Student 143
Are We Really Modeling? 146
Planning to Model for the Whole Class 147
Preparing to Be a Model 148
Modeling, Not Assigning 148
Admiring Trouble 149
- The "Trouble" 149
- Examining the "Trouble" With an Admiring Lens 150
- What I Did 151
- What I Learned 152

Conclusion 152

Andrew Levine Photography

CHAPTER EIGHT

Be a Mentor: Guiding Students to Try New Ways of Reading — 155

Being a Mentor — 156
Break Down Strategies Into Steps — 157
- Name One Step at a Time — 157
- Telling, Not Questioning — 158
- Focus on What to Do — 159
- Keep Prompts Clear — 160
- Over Time, Do Less — 161

Mentoring a Small Group of Readers — 162
Mentoring the Whole Class During a Read Aloud — 166
Admiring Trouble — 168
- The "Trouble" — 168
- Examining the "Trouble" With an Admiring Lens — 168
- What We Did — 168
- What I Learned — 170

Conclusion — 171

CHAPTER NINE

Teaching Students Strategies for How to Be Admirers — 173

How to Talk About Your Reading Process — 175
- Lesson 1: What Is a Reading Process? — 176
- Lesson 2: Using a Visual to Show the Process — 177
- Lesson 3: Learning the Language of Reading — 179

How to Set Goals for Yourself as a Reader — 179
- Lesson 4: Choosing From a Class List of Goals — 180
- Lesson 5: Creating Goals From Categories — 181
- Lesson 6: Create Personalized Goals — 182

How to Reflect on Your Mindset — 182
- Lesson 7: Using Read Alouds to Teach Mindset — 183
- Lesson 8: Analyzing Characters' Mindset — 184
- Lesson 9: Identifying Our Own Mindset as Readers — 185
- Lesson 10: Develop a Growth Mindset as a Reader — 186

How to Give Each Other Feedback — 187
- Lesson 11: Listen, Look, and Label (Without Opinions) — 188
- Lesson 12: Discuss the Outcome — 189

How to Ask for Support 189
   • Lesson 13: Getting Clear About What You Need   190
   • Lesson 14: Choosing Where to Get Support   191
Conclusion 192

Andrew Levine Photography

CHAPTER TEN

Embracing Curiosity:
Entry Points for Getting Started   195

Entry Point 1: Shift Roles 197
Entry Point 2: Shift Lenses From
   Deficit to Admiring 199
Entry Point 3: Shift Your Focus From
   the Teacher to Students 199
Entry Point 4: Shift Classroom Spaces 200
Entry Point 5: Shift Toward Feedback
   From Students 202
Entry Point 6: Shift Toward Feedback
   From Trusted Colleagues 202
Entry Point 7: Admire Yourself 203

Appendices

Appendix A. Student-Focused Reading Checklist   204
Appendix B. Continuum: How We Might Shift
   Our Instruction Toward Ownership   205
Appendix C. Chart of Balanced Literacy
   Reading Components   206

Reproducible Classroom Charts

Be a Miner 207
Be a Mirror 209
Be a Model 211
Be a Mentor 213

References   214

Index   218

Acknowledgments

Thank you to my partner John Altieri for inspiring me, reminding me students matter most, and modeling what it means to regard the world with wonder and awe. I am grateful for your support, guidance, and ideas about teaching, learning, living, and writing this book.

Thank you to my students. Every student I worked with as a classroom teacher, consultant, researcher, and auntie has taught me the importance of approaching children with curiosity. My teachers truly are the student readers who took the time to let me peek into their "reading minds" and shared a part of who they are with me. They all deserve to be seen with an admiring lens.

Thank you to my collaborators Gail Cordello, Chris Fuller, and Grace White for allowing me to work alongside you in your classrooms. Our time reflecting, questioning, and talking with children helped form the practices outlined in this book. Thank you for your passion, open-mindedness, and willingness to try things out, along with your unwavering trust in students.

Thank you to Corwin Literacy. My editor, Wendy Murray, offered tremendous support throughout the entire writing process. Wendy pushed my thinking, refined my writing, and helped me clarify my vision. I am very grateful for her efforts. Thank you to Lisa Luedeke, Maura Sullivan, Julie Nemer, and Emeli Warren for your teamwork on this book. Judy Wallis and Rosanne Kurstedt offered tremendous feedback as reviewers, and their ideas ultimately made this book much clearer. Andrew Levine followed me into a school and beautifully documented the ideas in this book with his photography.

Thank you to my teammates Julie Budzinski-Flores, Patty McGee, and Julie McAuley for supporting teachers in so many ways, allowing them to take on new roles, and helping to create classrooms where students own their learning.

Thank you to the teachers who contributed photographs and student work documented in this book. Thank you to Laura Sarsten, Pam Koutrakos, Ronnie Powers, Courtney Rejent, and Lena Guroian. I also appreciate the Speyer Legacy School and Sicomac School for allowing us to take photographs of their inspiring classrooms and students. I wish I could name each educator I have worked with across the years, for each of you taught me so much, whether it was the ways you sat talking to students about books, the extra time I saw you spend really connecting with your students long after the bell rang, or the tough questions you asked about what we could be doing that really works.

Thank you to my mentors Lucy Calkins and my former colleagues at TCRWP. This book builds on the work I did while a staff developer at the Teachers College Reading and Writing Project, which shaped much of my thinking about the teaching of reading. This book also stems from my early reading instruction experiences in the Boston Public Schools with master teachers Barbara McLaughlin and Malini Mayerhauser.

Thank you to my friend Renee Houser, my colleague and fellow iron woman, for all the brainstorming sessions while running and riding together.

Thank you to my family. My mom, Josette Lumbruno, and my dad, Gary Goldberg-O'Maxfield, raised me with an admiring lens. Your mindfulness has greatly impacted the ways I live my life as a teacher, reader, and writer.

CHAPTER ONE

Reading on One's Own

What We Really Mean by Take-Charge Independence

Andrew Levine Photography

"Wait. What are we supposed to do?" a student asked her teacher, who had just finished teaching a minilesson. Many students were opening their books and beginning to read, but a few sat there waiting for the teacher to tell them exactly what to do. Flash forward an hour to our planning meeting where the teacher asked her colleagues, "Wait. What are we supposed to do?" as she expressed concerns about student engagement and next steps for instruction. Many of us—both students and teachers—are asking this same question about **what we should be doing.** The complexity and ambiguity of teaching reading can lead us to feel overwhelmed and confused about what is right. While no one can answer the question about what you *are supposed* to do, I wrote this book to help answer the question, *What can we do*? This first chapter is meant to open up a conversation about what we and students really mean when we seek *independence*. What does independence really look like?

Teaching in general, and teaching reading in particular, is always going to be in flux as we seek to understand the relationships that support learning. We as practitioners are continually adapting and deepening our practice, and on a bigger canvas, new research findings influence classroom instruction. This research comes into our profession from the four corners of neuroscience, social psychology, science, and economics. As I write this book, I lean on findings from inside and outside the education field, as well as my own field research, and am aware that ideas I contribute are part of an ongoing conversation about **which practices matter most for readers and learners.**

John Hattie actually researched the research to identify the keepers. Hattie's 2012 study encompassed more than 240 million students; he identified qualities that did and did not support student achievement. To discover this, in essence, Hattie combed the prior research to pinpoint those instructional practices that really moved the needle on students' academic growth. One such finding is the degree to which effective teachers were able to identify student learning as opposed to mere compliance. He states, "For some, learning occurs if the students complete the task . . . and 'pass' the tests. Moving towards understanding learning, however, means starting with the private world of each student" (Hattie, 2012, p. 37). He goes on to say, **"The key is to understand what is going on in each student's mind"** (Hattie, 2012, p. 37). In other words, student compliance reveals who did and did not do the assignment, and who could and could not do it well. But understanding what students have learned reveals far more, because we really don't have clarity about what to teach next if we only see the end products of our assignments.

Hattie's language is evocative, and his findings are striking to me because teachers have this front-row seat from which to observe their students' processes, yet many of them struggle to know *how* to observe, how to access the "private world of each student." And with good reason—trying to understand students' learning process can feel like trying to find a secret door to the student's inner learner.

What are the mindsets and moves we need to find that door? This is the central question I seek to answer in this book. The short answer? We do a few things at once. **I'll first talk about stepping back so students can step forward.** When we step back, we can become admirers, and it's this vantage point that I want you to picture in your mind's eye as you read this book.

To admire means to regard with wonder and surprise (more on this in Chapter Three). In order to access **students' thinking, choices, and process, we need to take the time to get to know them well.** We can't just get the gist of who they are. Each day, we have the opportunity to study them. This means we approach readers as admirers with a few beliefs in mind:

- **All students are worthy of study and to be regarded with wonder.**
- **All students are readers, yet their processes may look different.**
- **All students can learn to make purposeful choices about their reading.**
- **All students can develop ownership of their reading lives.**

These beliefs help frame what it means to use an admiring lens as teachers. Our actions and beliefs—and, perhaps most significantly, our mindsets—can help us **get in our students' minds and better understand what and how they are learning.** The most effective reading teachers I know use an admiring lens when approaching students, and this lens impacts the roles they play.

Independent reading leads to engagement and achievement. Decades of research have proven that time spent reading has a significant impact on reading ability.

Gravity Goldberg

What Does It Really Mean to Read on One's Own?

PARTS OF A READING WORKSHOP

A group of literacy coaches and I stepped out from a fifth-grade classroom coaching session. Typically, when we finish classroom coaching sessions, we are bursting with lots to talk about, but this time we were all silent. At the time, I could not pinpoint what was going on, but I knew we all were a bit puzzled and confused. The classroom we worked in was one that uses a Reading Workshop model for instruction (see the Parts of a Reading Workshop visual below). Each day, the teacher offers a brief minilesson where she shows a strategy; then the students go off to read on their own and use the strategies that have been taught. As the students are reading, the teacher has individual or small group conferences to check in with students, assess their progress, and offer feedback. This particular fifth-grade class had all of the structures of typical Reading Workshop classrooms in place. The minilesson was short, there were anchor charts, the students had books of their own choosing, the teacher moved around the room having conferences, and she even took notes on each one. If we were using a workshop structures checklist, we would have checked off every box. These students read for thirty or so minutes on their own. This is what we had just observed:

Gail sat at the class meeting area in front of her class of twenty-five fifth graders. She took out a familiar book and showed the students how she inferred the main character's conflict. She opened up the book and explained the strategy. The students smiled and turned to tell their reading partners what they had just seen in the minilesson. The teacher finished her explanation and said, "Now today you are all going to go back to your seats and infer the character's conflict in the novels you are each reading."

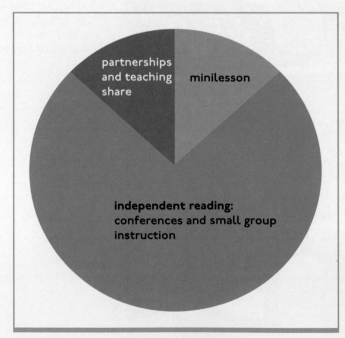

Parts of a Reading Workshop

Gail pointed to an organizer that was projected and discussed during the lesson. "Remember to fill out your copy of this chart when you find the character's conflict. Now please go begin your independent reading." She smiled and stood up to show the students it was time to begin working.

Immediately following the minilesson, the students arose quietly, walked to their desks, and took out their independent reading books. Each student made sure to pick up a blank conflict organizer on the way to his or her seat and began by filling in the title and author. Gail walked over to Tyler first. Tyler is a tall and lanky boy who was just beginning a new book that day. He was reading the back blurb and looking at the cover when Gail approached him.

"Tyler, are you thinking about the conflict?" Gail asked.

"Not yet," he responded. "But I will as soon as I start reading."

"OK. Great. Thank you." Gail stood up and walked across the room. The entire class was pin-drop quiet as students read.

Gail stopped and squatted next to Sam. "Sam, can you tell me about your book?" she asked. Sam began to retell important parts of his book. He was almost at the end and seemed to want to quickly get done with his conversation with Gail so he could finish the book. "So I noticed you have not written anything on your conflict organizer yet," Gail noted.

"Yeah, well, I just want to finish my book, and then I will go back and do that," he explained.

"Do you know what the conflict is? Can you tell me so I know that you understand?" she asked.

Sam began explaining several conflicts in the book and how most of them were resolved and how he just wanted to see how it would all end. Gail checked off the box "infers character conflict" on her conference checklist and then thanked Sam and stood up to work with the next student.

By the end of the reading period, Gail had conferred with five students about character conflict, knowing she would meet with five more per day until she'd conferred with each student. Before the period ended, she said, "Now readers, please find your reading partner and use your organizer to explain the conflict." Each set of students found one another and began sharing their organizers and telling about their books.

At the end of the period, during a transition time, I had a few minutes to speak with some of Gail's students. I was curious to hear their perspectives on reading.

"So how is reading going for you?" I asked a triad of students.

All three students shrugged their shoulders.

"What have you learned about how to read?"

"We learned how to infer the character's conflict today," Tyler explained.

"I noticed that was today's minilesson topic. How did it go for you?" I inquired.

"I was just starting the first page of my book today, so it was kinda hard to figure out the conflict," Tyler acknowledged.

I thought about what he had just said. It was not really applicable or helpful for Tyler to be asked to infer conflict as he was just starting a novel. At the start of a book, most readers first need to figure out who the characters are and where they are, and then get into the world the author has created. Many books do not start off with the conflict on the first page. The assignment felt forced. Tyler tried to use the strategy because the teacher told him to and not because he needed it right then.

"What about you, Sam?" I asked. Now I was curious as to whether this strategy helped him today.

"I already knew the conflicts in my book because I was at the end. I wrote them down on the worksheet after I finished the book. I loved this book!" he replied.

"So did the conflict *worksheet* help you with your understanding of this book today?" I tend to ask these sorts of reflective questions of students to figure out not just what they did but also how it went. I noticed that rather than an organizer he called it a worksheet—something to prove to the teacher he did his work.

"No. I just wrote it down because the teacher told us to. I already knew the conflicts," he honestly answered.

By the time I spoke to the third student in this group, I was really starting to think about how the students in this class can follow directions well, but they may not actually be fully owning their reading processes. I asked Carla, the other student in this group, "What did you work on today in your reading?"

"I worked on character conflicts too. That was the minilesson. I got the assignment done quickly, though, so I could get to reading and enjoying my book," she proudly stated.

"So, the work you did, the assignment, did not help you enjoy your book?" I wanted to clarify.

She actually rolled her eyes at me and smirked. "No."

"Hmm," I thought. Something was getting in the way of students driving their own reading experiences. I had at least one idea to discuss with my colleague Gail.

A few years earlier, prior to implementing Reading Workshop, the students in this district had a very different instructional reading experience. At that time, most of the students' reading materials were chosen by the teachers or from an anthology, very little reading was done in class, and every book was tested after completing novel guides and worksheets. There was one period a week where students "just read" a book of their choosing. This team of literacy coaches had worked tirelessly alongside energetic and enthusiastic teachers who all wanted to get reading instruction right. They spent a few years putting structures in place so students had much more time each day to read on their own in school. They had read Allington's (2012) research on increasing the time spent with eyes on text, matching students to appropriate-level books, and the importance of comprehension instruction. They brought me in as a literacy consultant to help them create a reading curriculum that aligned with standards and used a balanced literacy model. We had been rolling up our sleeves over the past few years to build leveled classroom libraries, create meeting areas, and demonstrate Reading Workshop lessons to show what these structures look like. In those first few years, our goals for reading classrooms focused on organization, timing, and structures (see the Reading Workshop Checklist on the next page).

Now, sitting at our meeting table, the literacy coaches and I sat down and waited for the teacher, Gail, to join us. Gail walked in, and before she even sat down,

Reading Workshop Checklist

- [ ] The teacher has created an organized and leveled classroom library.
- [ ] The teacher's minilesson is short (about seven to ten minutes).
- [ ] The teacher has created a class meeting area with anchor charts.
- [ ] The teacher meets daily with students in conferences and small groups.
- [ ] The teacher takes notes during conferences.
- [ ] There is time each day for students to read on their own.

she said, "*Something is off!* It is like they are doing everything I ask of them, but . . ." Her voice trailed off. "I guess I want more than that. How do we get them to use strategies when I am not telling them to? Now that would really mean they were learning to be readers!" We all let out a big sigh and nodded.

What we were seeking is what Stephanie Harvey calls active literacy. She explains, "Classrooms that promote active literacy fairly burst with enthusiastic and engaged learners . . . They can't get away with being passive participants when they are the ones doing the thinking" (Harvey & Goudvis, 2007, p. 16). Gail and her colleagues realized something needed to shift for this sort of active literacy to happen.

So what was going on?

Examining Teacher Roles

Together Gail, the literacy coaches, and I began looking closely at the roles she was taking on in the classroom. We recapped what she did in each main part of the Reading Workshop period that day. In the beginning of the lesson, Gail gave an assignment—to locate the character's conflict and write it down. Gail and I noticed that the minilesson narrowed the students' focus solely on character conflict and did not leave room for other types of thinking that likely would help the varied readers in her classroom. Giving an assignment also created a notion that reading a novel is about completing a task and creating a product rather than about "constructing meaning in an active, ongoing process" (Barnhouse, 2014, p. 30). When we assign, we send the message that reading is done for someone else and to meet another person's expectations. We know that reading is a deeply personal act—one that varies from reader to reader depending on the person, the text, and the context (Freire, 1970; Goldberg & Serravallo, 2007). Gail realized she had become the assigner in the opening part of the period.

The second role Gail took on was that of a monitor. Gail did walk around and meet with students, but as we all debriefed, she realized she had been quite focused on making sure the students did what they were told. She admitted she felt this constant internal pressure to keep the students focused on the assignment even when it was not applicable. Teachers often feel this pressure because it can be difficult to assess how students are doing with the curriculum. Checking that they have addressed the minilesson topic each day often ends up a default behavior. We know that students never fit in our checkboxes and are much more than a list of skills to be demonstrated, yet the push for data can lead us to use conferring time as monitoring and checking time.

A third role that Gail assumed was that of a manager and decision maker. Gail, like many of us, feels the weight of responsibility for many students, the curriculum, and the standards they have to meet. It is understandable that she felt the need to make most of the decisions for her students. After all, it is much quicker and more efficient for teachers to manage the choices themselves. The problem with using efficiency as a goal is that it often creates passive readers who sit and wait to get directions, and eventually are so accustomed to being told exactly what to do that they don't self-start their own reading and learning tasks. Why is this passivity corrosive? Because it's not how authentic learning operates. Authentic learning takes more will and muscle, so to speak. For example, when I sit and read an article at my desk, no one is there to tell me what to do and how to read. Or when I'm reclining on a couch on a Sunday, trying to untangle a complex mystery novel, I set the rules for how long I read, whether I flip back or forward for clues, and whether I take time to read the details about the physical landscape or not. As someone who has in a sense earned the right to read on my own, I call the shots, and it's this very independence with the myriad choices I need to make as I read that gives me the drive to exert a lot of mental energy on a Sunday afternoon.

As teachers, we can begin to set students on the road to this kind of agency by thinking about how we can teach readers to make purposeful decisions for themselves. One place to begin this reflection is to look at the language that rides along with being an assigner, a monitor, and a manager.

Peter Johnston, the literacy and language researcher, points out in *Opening Minds* (2012) that the language we use with our students positions us in different relationships with them. "Teaching is planned opportunism. We have an idea of what we want to teach children, and we plan ways to make that learning possible. When we put our plans into action, children offer us opportunities to say something, or not, and the choices we make affect what happens next" (Johnston, 2012, p. 4). Johnston teaches us so much about the power of productive talk—about learning to know when to say something, what to say, and when to be still and quiet—so that children can have more room and voice in that moment.

It is not just our language but also our *actions*, *decisions*, and *beliefs* that shape the roles we play in our classrooms and color how students perceive their own agency. Our language gets bundled with our actions.

I am modeling a reading strategy during a whole class read aloud. When modeling, I reveal my actions, thinking, decisions, and mindsets to students. Young readers benefit greatly from an awareness of growth mindset.

John Altieri

The assigner: When we are the assigners, we often end up telling students exactly what to do and when to do it. This role results in students completing our assignments. While on the surface this might sound like what we want, it may not be helpful for students for three main reasons. First, not all students need to do the same thing in the same way at the same time. Second, it fosters dependence on us as teachers. Finally, our assignments can inhibit authentic reading experiences that lead to greater student learning and motivation.

The monitor: If we play the role of the monitor, we run the risk of too much time being spent checking that every student has completed the task. This often results in students trying to prove to us they did the assignment well. Proving to us becomes the goal, not necessarily learning. When we are monitors, we are limiting the choices students have to create and find their own ways of reading. It also narrows our vision so we are only looking and checking the task of that day. Think about how much we might be missing. All of this monitoring and checking takes so much time that we lose out on time to individualize and get to know readers well enough to meet them where they are.

The manager: When we go on autopilot in the role of manager, we make choices for the students and tell them what, where, how, and when to read. We have all of the control, which leaves students merely following our directions. While following directions might sound like something we want our students to do, it can have potentially negative consequences. First, the teacher's choices may not be right for every student. Second, students may not learn to make choices for themselves, thus creating a model of dependency in the classroom. Third, we know that choice is linked to increases in motivation (National Council of Teachers of English, 2009). If we make all of the choices, we may end up decreasing our students' motivation and ownership. The chart on the next page shows how teacher roles and actions impact student behaviors.

Taking the Spotlight Off the Teacher

After discussing Gail's roles, one literacy coach remarked that our entire conversation had focused on the teacher. "Gail did this, and Gail did that," she said. "It's all the teacher's behaviors."

I glanced back at our Reading Workshop Checklist and noticed none of the items on the list were focused on the students. I was aghast. In our efforts to create classrooms where students read on their own, we had largely forgotten about the students.

Teacher Roles	Teacher Actions	Resulting Student Behaviors	Why It May Not Be Helpful
Assigner	Tell students exactly what to do and when to do it	• Complete assignments • Read within the bounds of expectations • Do the minimal amount of work	• Not all students need to do the same thing in the same way or at the same time • Fosters dependence • Can inhibit authentic reading experiences • May habitually prevent creative or original thinking
Monitor	Check that every student has done the task	• Prove they did the assignment well • Look to the teacher to tell them how they did • Meet others' expectations for them • Compare themselves to the class norm • Confuse completing tasks with learning	• Limits choices for the students to create their own ways of reading • Narrows the teacher's vision to solely look and check • Can take up so much time the teacher cannot individualize and teach
Manager	Make choices for the students and tell them what, where, how, and when	• Follow directions • Wait for others to solve problems for them • Waste time waiting for the teacher to decide for them	• The teacher's choices may not be right for every student • Students do not learn to make choices • Creates dependency • Can decrease motivation and ownership • Doesn't help students develop the disposition to generate choices and decisions of their own regarding texts

Common Teacher Roles and Possible Unintended Consequences

I remembered a recent weekend at a professional soccer game. During the game, I watched the players, cheered for goals, groaned at missed opportunities, and stood up for close calls. I admired the players' every move. I did not once look over at the bench and watch the coach. I do know the coach had a lot to do with how the players did that day, but my attention was on the field. I don't go to soccer games to ignore the players, yet I could not help but think we were doing this very thing in our reading classrooms. We were focused on the teacher and missing the readers—really missing what matters most. We were observing Gail's teaching but not the readers in the room.

Category	Student-Focused Observations
Classroom environment	☐ Students refer to charts and choose when and how to use them. ☐ Students can select from libraries that reflect their levels and interests. ☐ Students use spaces for whole group, small group, and individual work. ☐ Students use materials independently and choose them when needed.
Student engagement	☐ Students read for the entire independent reading time. ☐ Students regularly collaborate in partnerships or book clubs. ☐ Students think, discuss, and articulate their learning. ☐ Students work through challenges and confidently choose strategies to use when needed.
Individualization	☐ Students regularly participate in either conferences or small group work. ☐ Students' unique strengths and needs are used in conference decisions. ☐ Students are focused and independent. ☐ Students choose their own goals and self-assess their progress.
Independence and transfer	☐ Students transfer teaching points to novel experiences. ☐ Students use strategies several days or even months after they were first taught. ☐ Students can explain their goals, strengths, and next steps as a reader. ☐ Students do not look for the teacher to solve problems or answer questions. ☐ Students can explain what they are doing and why.

Student-Focused Reading Checklist

I asked the group, "What if we made a new checklist where all of the items are about what students are doing? Let's try this and see what we find." The Student-Focused Reading Checklist, shown on the previous page, is what we created, and it ended up being very helpful in our ongoing work together.

After creating this second, reader-focused checklist, we began to get excited, and now we couldn't stop talking. At the end of that conversation, we realized that the workshop that we'd set in motion up till now had established only one facet of what a Reading Workshop really is—a place in which students read on their own. The "off" part was that although the students were reading on their own, their experience of the text was being framed by the teacher's agenda, and they simply copied what Gail did. They did just enough and seemed to see the purpose of Reading Workshop as pleasing their teacher.

We seemed to be still missing what reading researcher and scholar P. David Pearson (2011) describes as *transfer*. By *transfer*, Pearson means that in comprehension instruction, *when* and *how* students apply the strategies is key. Students need to be taught in a manner that they know to apply strategies in new reading situations, with unfamiliar texts. Only then can we say with assurance that their comprehension abilities have improved. We realized the students needed to own their reading, which means much more than just time to read on their own. Because we focused so much on the teacher and the classroom structures, we had somehow lost sight of the readers. As I collaborated and supported other districts across the country, I found this same pattern. We gave it a name that day with Gail, but it certainly was not unique to her classroom.

The Facets of Ownership

Owning your reading means being an initiator of your own intentions as a reader. It is being engaged and feeling in charge of your purpose and process of reading. Nell K. Duke and P. David Pearson (2001) point out that while there are many factors that affect students' ability to comprehend texts, a primary factor is their motivation, purpose, goals, and engagement with the texts and experiences. "As teachers of literacy, we must have as an instructional goal, regardless of age, grade or achievement level, the development of students as purposeful, engaged, and ultimately independent comprehenders" (Duke & Pearson, 2001, p. 423). Sheridan Blau (2003), a professor of English education at Teachers College, Columbia University, explains that students need what he calls performative literacy—a set of dispositions that help a reader construct knowledge and fully function in the twenty-first century. Performative literacy requires students to "become more active, responsible and responsive readers than ever before" (Blau, 2003, p. 19). One of these dispositions is "a capacity to monitor and direct one's own reading process" (Blau, 2003, p. 21).

Stephanie Harvey and Smokey Daniels (2009) explain the importance of choice being woven into the way the curriculum is written and implemented in their book, *Comprehension and Collaboration: Inquiry Circles in Action*. They explain that classrooms where deep comprehension happens are ones where "students are exercising choice in topics, reading, and ways to show their learning, but this is not a temporary treat or a 'day off' from the official curriculum" (Harvey & Daniels, 2009, p. 6). In other words, students are in charge of their reading and develop ownership of what, how, and why they read in the curriculum and in their daily practices.

Initiating, knowing one's intentions, one's purpose, one's goals—these are all facets of owning reading. In this light, engagement and motivation are the emotional/psychological states that result from ownership. Thus, ownership should always

This is a self-directed reader. He selected his book and his reading spot. He chose what he is working on as he reads, and has clear reasons why. He's part of a classroom culture wherein students make purposeful decisions that lead to growth.

Gravity Goldberg

be part of the professional conversation about motivation and engagement—and perhaps addressed first because, until students have that sense of autonomy, they can't be fully engaged. To do otherwise is to put the cart before the horse.

My dissertation research (Goldberg, 2010) allowed me to spend an entire year observing in an English classroom, interviewing students, trying to understand the transition the class was attempting to make from a more teacher-centered model to one with more student choice and ownership. I found that many students were stuck in compliant ways of reading on their own, spending each day following directions and completing reading assignments.

While the study's results cannot be generalized, I hear and see similar patterns in my work in schools throughout the country. Many students are not transferring what they learned during reading time into science reading, or historical reading, or even home reading. So in addition to a lack of engagement, we've got a lack of real learning—for without transfer, there is no deep learning. In fact, many students are reading as little as possible to get by and please the teacher, and get the A. I ended up calling the "something is off" realization from Gail's classroom the "ownership crisis."

The choice to use the word *crisis* was not an easy one. I chose it because the lack of ownership feels so prevalent and so pervasive and very few educators know what to do. Crisis is a time when a difficult or important decision must be made. I think we are in such a time. In meetings, in classroom coaching sessions, in parent conferences, and in honest talks with students, we all seem to be noticing the same thing. Most students do not own their learning. William Deresiewicz, Yale University professor and author of *Excellent Sheep: The Miseducation of the American Elite and the Way to a Meaningful Life* (2014), explains, "The problem is that students have been taught that that is all that education is: doing your homework, getting the answers, acing the test . . . They've learned to 'be a student,' not to use their minds" (p. 13). Deresiewicz goes on to explain the repercussions of teaching students to comply and work hard simply for the purpose of getting an A. He claims college students and recent graduates are more depressed, are more anxious, and feel a lack of meaning in their lives as a result of this type of education.

I think it's fair to say that many teachers in elementary schools would not name the crisis in terms of their students' compliance. In my experience, the concern is expressed along the lines of questions like this: "What about the students who don't use the strategies on their own?" or "How do I get them to care about their reading?" or "I just don't know what to do. These students just don't put the work in, and it shows. How can you help me?"

How Rigor Fits In

In the clamor for rigor, we need to remember that students only become rigorous readers if they do more, think more, read more, and initiate more of their learning. You can't rigorously read a text unless you bring your own vigor to it. The work of understanding an author's intended meaning is intense, and the part that hasn't gotten enough airtime in professional discussions of late is students' drive and agency, as they work through a text. Beneath the national call for rigor in our students is not so much a hope for students meeting higher expectations or a desire to see students break out in a sweat over a challenging text. Underneath it all is a wish to see a stronger appetite for learning. When we say we want rigor, there is something wistful at work: We want vigor. We want ownership.

Students deserve an education that goes well beyond teaching them to comply. Let's instead create environments that support students who are actively engaged and have ownership of their reading. The current educational and global context requires students to be innovative, creative, and invested so they can succeed in the jobs of the future. But they can't become these qualities unless they love to learn, and loving to do something means that you love to do it on your own, of your own volition, and you practice it and master it to the point that you really do "own" the expertise. Ownership will set students up to take on tomorrow's environmental and cultural challenges, and the challenge of creating access and equality for more and more people on the planet (Godin, 2012; Robinson & Aronica, 2009). The following chart shows the difference in choices in compliant classrooms and reader-owned classrooms.

Choices in Compliant Classrooms	Choices in Reader-Owned Classrooms
• To do what you are told or not • To do it the teacher's way or not	• What to read • Purpose for reading • How to write about reading • How to talk about reading • Goals for self as a reader

Choices in Compliant Versus Reader-Owned Classrooms

The Pitfalls of Turning Play Into Work: Motivation Challenges

In *Drive: The Surprising Truth About What Motivates Us*, Daniel Pink (2009) recounts decades-old research on narrowly focusing on rewards and punishments—on getting people to comply. Most schools and businesses are built on the "carrots and sticks" structure of motivation. Carrots are the dangling rewards, and sticks are the consequences if the person does not comply. In reading classrooms, the carrots might be attention, extra time in a choice activity, or a good grade. Reading Workshop approaches were meant to move away from rewards—books, stickers, points, pizzas, and so on—but lo and behold, even the seemingly greater authenticity of a workshop approach is often caught in the old paradigm. The chart on the next page shows how typical reading instructional practices often get distorted and what we can do to keep them more vital.

The sticks might be completing a task, an assignment, or doing what is told. Most teachers were told that this is the way to get students to obey us and learn. But, as Pink points out, this form of motivation can actually backfire and lead to less motivation and engagement. When classrooms turn something intrinsically motivating into the teacher's goal that will be rewarded, the activity is viewed as work and loses its intrinsic motivation. This is called the Sawyer Effect and is focused on how there are hidden costs of rewards.

One particular set of studies stands out to me as an educator. Lepper, Greene, and Nisbett (1973), three behavioral scientists, studied preschool students during their free-play portion of the school day. They found that the drawing area was a favorite, and many students chose this activity. As part of the study, they wanted to see what would happen when drawing, an intrinsically motivating and fun activity, was rewarded by the teachers. The teachers introduced to half of the class a "good player" certificate that students could earn from choosing the drawing activity. These students would be rewarded for choosing to draw. Guess what happened? After two weeks, the number of students who chose to participate in drawing went down dramatically in the group that was told they would get a reward for it. These results were further support for the Sawyer Effect. Drawing (play) was turned into work and no longer viewed as intrinsically valuable. To quote Pink (2009), "Careful consideration of reward effects reported in 128 experiments led to the conclusion that tangible rewards tend to have a substantially negative effect on intrinsic motivation" (p. 39).

Practice	What Tends to Get Distorted	How to Keep It Vital
Writing in reading notebooks	• Students write about their reading in the same ways all year. • Students view writing about reading as a task for the teacher. • Writing about reading becomes an activity that may get in the way of time spent reading and thinking.	• Discuss why readers authentically write about their reading. • Model a variety of ways you write about your reading for authentic reasons. • Invite students to invent and share a variety of ways of writing about their reading. • Remind students to connect reading notebook entries to the reader's purpose.

Using reading logs to record number of pages, minutes, and books read	• Students regard volume and recording data as the goal of reading.
	• Students lie about how much they have read.
	• Students choose "easy" or short books that can be read quickly.
	• Completing books is confused with understanding and enjoying books.
	• The log can become an accountability measure rather than a reflective tool.
		• Connect reading logs to students' individually set goals.
		• Show students how to use the data they are collecting to reflect on their reading lives.
		  ○ Am I choosing books I enjoy?
		  ○ Am I giving myself a variety of reading experiences?
		  ○ Am I challenging myself as a reader?
		• Discuss why readers might read more on some days than others and create spaces for honest discussions about why we might read more and deeper in certain experiences.

(Continued)

Practice	What Tends to Get Distorted	How to Keep It Vital
Using reading logs to record number of pages, minutes, and books read *(continued)*		• Rather than making the reading log a yearlong "accountability" tool, it can be used sporadically when readers want to gather more information about themselves.
Using checklists in our reading conferences	• We look at students as boxes to be checked. • Our vision gets narrowed, and we miss a lot about readers' practices. • Students focus on proving to us they can use a skill on our list. • Skills are practiced but not necessarily chosen when needed or useful.	• Start conferences with a question or category in mind and get more specific with your observations over time. • Take anecdotal notes to recall unique behaviors, interactions, and individualized noticings. • Use a variety of recording tools to remember what you uncovered about students' inner reading world (photos, notes, artifacts, etc.) and possibly involve them in this process. • Remember to approach students openly, not focusing on what you found the last time you were with them. Who are they as readers today?

(Continued) appears at top of table.

Workshop Practices: How They May Become Ossified

I keep thinking about teachers' checklists of reading skills and how reading might unintentionally be turned into work and not be pleasurable for its own sake. When we tell students they will be rewarded with something external for reading or punished for not reading, we are putting the emphasis on something external, and we are accidentally divorcing the act of reading from its intrinsic value. When I sit down to read at night, it is not for a grade or sticker but because I find pleasure in the experience of reading. It has intrinsic value for me. Even when reading on their own, students may view reading as "work" and not play—something to be completed for someone else. When readers have ownership, they view the work that is often a part of reading as play. By play, I mean something with intrinsic value in and of itself.

Peter Gray, an evolutionary developmental psychologist and professor at Boston College, studies the impact play has on children and warns of the consequences of our children being robbed of the freedoms that help them really learn. He explains, "Children are designed, by nature, to play and explore on their own, independently of adults. They need freedom in order to develop; without it they suffer" (Gray, 2013, p. 4). He goes on to explain how lack of freedom kills the spirit and stunts mental growth: "The school system has directly and indirectly, often unintentionally, fostered an attitude in society that children learn and progress primarily by doing tasks that are directed and evaluated by adults, and that children's own activities are wasted time" (Gray, 2013, p. 8). The results are often superficial knowledge and many missed opportunities for deeper learning to happen. When students are taking charge of their own learning by making choices about all aspects of their reading lives, they are using the freedom associated with play to develop a deeper appreciation for reading and the ability to read.

What's Next?

In Chapter Two, I examine why grit and mindset are vital elements to consider when making choices about what supports we want to offer our readers. Once I unpack why these traits are so important, I explain new roles that reading teachers can take on. When teachers shift their roles, there is space for readers to develop the ownership and agency they need for true learning. I also take us back into Gail's classroom to see how she shifted into these new roles and as a result her students owned more of their reading lives.

CHAPTER TWO

Shifting Roles

Be a Miner, a Mirror, a Model, a Mentor

In Chapter One, I described the typical teacher roles of being an assigner, a monitor, and a manager along with the possible unintended consequences. These consequences include a lack of student ownership, transfer, and compliance rather than learning. In this chapter, I explain why students need to struggle, become risk takers, and develop growth mindsets. When we shift our teacher roles, we create space for these qualities to be developed in our students. We've heard the terms *grit* and *mindset*, and in this chapter, I unpack what they mean and how they can impact our reading instruction.

The Gift of Problems: Creating a Willingness to Struggle

We are suffering from an epidemic of helpfulness. Children are constantly being helped by adults with everything from tying their shoes to figuring out the meaning of a Shakespearean sonnet. We are so afraid to let our students struggle that we have made it our job to make sure it rarely ever happens. This need to

Andrew Levine Photography

constantly help our students comes from a well-intentioned place, but it does not foster growth and maturity. When we step in during a problem or struggle and save the day for our students, we are not being helpful; we are actually robbing them of their evolutionary right to become problem solvers.

David Rock, in his book *Quiet Leadership* (2006), explains what happens in the brain when people solve their own problems. His book draws upon the research done by Jeff Hawkins on how the brain is hardwired to create maps. When people encounter a problem they need to solve and go on to struggle to figure out a solution, a synapse is being formed in the brain. That is basically a connection from one area to the next. The brain actually builds a new map and gets smarter. As this synapse is forming and the solution has arrived, there is a "lightbulb moment," a feeling of eureka. This eureka feeling is actually a release of chemicals that are being produced by the brain—dopamine, adrenaline, and serotonin. These chemicals give you a high feeling as wonderful sensations arrive in your body. We have all experienced the learner's high. This is a topic researched by Csikszentmihalyi in his book *Flow* (1990) that looks at how we can enter optimal performance zones.

When we step in and help our students solve a problem, we are actually stealing their high. We mean well. We think we are being helpful, but in fact we have robbed our students of two important evolutionary and learning experiences. First, we have not let them form the synapse in the brain that forms true learning and connections. Second, we have not let them have the high of problem solving, which is designed to reinforce their motivation to problem-solve in the future. Being helpful often makes the helper feel better, not the one being helped, because we stole the learner's high. As teachers, we may inadvertently be walking around high on the dopamine, adrenaline, and serotonin we get from solving our students' problems.

Paul Tough's book, *How Children Succeed* (2013), examines the character traits that impact student success and includes interviews with experts in the field of character education. Tough explains, "What kids need more than anything is a little hardship; some challenges, some deprivation that they can overcome, even if just to prove to themselves that they can" (p. 84). This claim is based on Dan Kindlon's (2000) research as a professor of psychology at Harvard University (Kindlon & Thompson, 2000), and Tough's interviews with school leaders at elite private high schools. Tough (2013) goes on to explain, "The best way for a young person to build character is for him to attempt something where there is a real and serious possibility of failure" so he can "achieve real and original success" (p. 85). Tough's work also stems from the research done on grit.

Angela Duckworth, the founder and lead researcher at the University of Pennsylvania's Duckworth Lab, studies how the character traits of self-control and grit impact people's lives. One important finding is the predictive power of grit to determine future success. Grit is defined as "perseverance and passion for long-term goals. Grit entails working strenuously toward challenges, maintaining effort and interest over years despite failure, adversity, and plateaus in progress" (Duckworth, Peterson, Matthews, & Kelly, 2007, p. 1087). In other words, students who have more grit are likely to see struggle as a vital part of the learning process and a natural part of working toward their goals.

Duckworth explains,

> Grit predicts surviving the arduous first summer of training at West Point and reaching the final rounds of the National Spelling Bee (Duckworth et al., 2007), . . . retention and performance among novice teachers (Duckworth, Quinn, & Seligman, 2009; Robertson-Kraft & Duckworth, 2014) . . . and graduation from Chicago public high schools (Eskreis-Winkler et al., 2014), over and beyond domain-relevant talent measures such as IQ, SAT or standardized achievement test scores, and physical fitness. (Duckworth Lab, 2015)

This research on grit has led to partnerships with educators and school districts to better understand how grit can be cultivated in students since it has a big impact on success.

One school partnership project includes explaining to students how learning grows from grit. "For instance, individuals who believe that frustration and confusion mean they should quit what they are doing may be taught that these emotions are common during the learning process. Likewise, individuals who believe that mistakes are to be avoided at all costs may be taught that the most effective form of practice entails tackling challenges beyond one's current skill level" (Duckworth Lab, 2015). Grit is developed by understanding that struggle is normal, needed, and helpful for growth toward goals.

John Hattie's research on academic growth and teaching is linked to psychologists' findings about character traits. "There are certainly many things that inspired teachers do *not* do: they do not use grading as punishment; they do not conflate behavioral and academic performance; they do not elevate quiet compliance over academic work; they do not excessively use worksheets . . . they do not evaluate their impact by compliance, covering the curriculum . . . and they do not prefer perfection . . . over risk-taking that involves mistakes" (Hattie, 2012,

p. 36). Hattie's research of what actually impacts student achievement supports the need for reader ownership. This is not just about making students feel good; this is also a way to ensure real, visible learning is going on. In order for real learning to occur, readers benefit from ownership that allows them to take risks, struggle, and continue to develop grit within a classroom that supports students without robbing them of their opportunities for struggle.

Shifting Roles Toward Reader Ownership

Recall the teacher, Gail, from Chapter One who wanted more for her students. Gail and her colleagues spent the rest of that school year reflecting with me and with their students about what was off. They set goals for themselves and with their students around fostering more reader ownership. Let's take a step back into Gail's classroom later in the year. Notice how she decided to take on very

Gail models her reading process in a whole class minilesson. This is not an assignment for students to complete right away. She is showing one way she thinks about characters, and expects her students to try it when the need for it arises in the books they are reading.

Gravity Goldberg

different roles with her students and creates space for students to own their reading lives. This involved a conscious shifting of her roles in the classroom so her students would assign, monitor, and manage their own reading. The following continuum shows the relationships between teacher, students, and each of their roles.

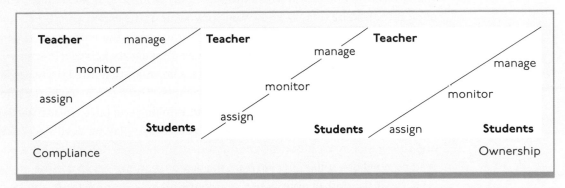

A Continuum: How We Might Shift Our Instruction Toward Ownership

Gail met her students in the meeting area and sat down with a pile of the books she was reading. She began by explaining what she was seeing in the classroom during reading time. "I have been noticing that many of you are beginning to write about the characters in your books in different ways. Colin drew a sketch of the character in his book and then labeled parts to remember the character's traits. Jose created a chart with a column for each character and space underneath to keep track of his thinking. Barb created this visual that connects the character's actions with a trait." Gail held up each student's example as she spoke to the class. She went on to remind her students that there are many ways to get to know a character and learn from his or her experiences.

Next, Gail modeled for the class how she plays devil's advocate with a claim she previously made about a character by stopping to reread the claim, thinking about if there is another way to view the character besides her initial reaction. Gail explained how she originally believed that Verbena in the novel *As Simple as It Gets* (Weeks, 2011) was immature, but as she read on, she pushed herself to rethink this. She showed the students how she could see more than one way to interpret a character's choices in a book. Now she also saw Verbena as seeking her own identity and struggling to understand the type of person she wanted to be. She explained that maybe Verbena was not just immature but rather moving from being a child to a teenager and resisting the changes that come from this. The class nodded as she showed her real, authentic strategy for pushing her thinking in new ways.

Gail ended the minilesson by mentoring students in how to make purposeful choices for reading time. "I know some of you are at the end of your books and already have many ideas about what you learned from the characters' experiences. You may want to spend some time today thinking about bigger lessons you learned across the book." She pointed to an anchor chart that listed strategies for learning from characters' choices and experiences. "Some of you are in the middle of your books and want to continue with thinking you have already started, or maybe you want to try what I showed you today—playing devil's advocate and trying to see your idea from another side." She pointed to her own book and reading notebook still on her lap from the demonstration. "And for those of you who are at the start of your books, you know many ways to get into the story and get to know the major elements, to clarify confusions, and to start forming ideas." She paused. "Take a minute to think about where you are in your book, the thinking you have already started, and set an intention for how you want to spend your reading time today. When you have decided, get going." She smiled as a few students immediately went off to their reading spots while others flipped through their reading notebooks and thought about their intentions. Gail knew they just needed a bit of time to make a choice.

Since the students in this class were spread out throughout the room in self-selected reading spots to help them stay focused, Gail took a moment to observe the students. She did not immediately begin checking what they were doing but instead focused on a student she was curious about. Gail walked over to Kristen and asked, "Do you mind if I interrupt you?" Kristen took a moment to finish reading the page and then looked up to greet her teacher. Over the next few moments, Gail asked, "What is your intention today as a reader?" and "How is it going for you?" to get insight into what Kristen wanted to work on and how she was approaching it. Kristen was at the beginning of a book, so the conference did not focus on the minilesson topic of playing devil's advocate. Also, since Kristen's intention was to figure out more about the setting of her book (a dystopian novel), Gail decided to focus on this. She asked Kristen why she had this intention, and Kristen explained that since this was her first time reading this book, she was confused about the setting, and because she had read many other dystopian novels, she knew setting was crucial for understanding the plot. Kristen set the agenda, and Gail spent time uncovering how she was reading, giving feedback on what she noticed, and then teaching her other ways of envisioning the setting—a crucial element in dystopian literature.

As Gail moved around the room, she conferred with a few more students, and each conference focused on a different topic, depending on each reader's intentions and needs. At the end of the period, Gail invited students to reflect and make one more choice. "Since there are about five minutes left in the period, take a moment to decide if you want to write a bit about your thinking or talk to your partner." Several students gathered with their partners. Some explained how they used their reading time, what they learned, and what they were left thinking about. Some showed their partners notes in their reading notebook and then used them as talking points to get feedback on their ideas. A few sat alone writing in their notebooks to get some closure on their thinking.

What Shifted?

This is not Gail's classroom; it is the readers' classroom. The readers own the learning. Gail's students read on their own throughout the reading period, but they did much more than comply. In fact, ownership was built into every aspect of the classroom experience and expectations. The students had choices of what to read, what to focus on, and how they would read. Students led conferences about their intentions and needs. Students were using strategies when they were needed, not simply mimicking the strategy shown that day, regardless of whether it applied or helped.

Gail's transformed classroom reminds me of something Theodore Levitt, an economist and Harvard professor, said: You don't go to the hardware store to buy a drill. You go because you need to put a hole in something. This analogy is useful as we think about why we apply reading strategies: You don't think about conflict because the teacher taught it that day; you think about conflict to understand character motivations. A strategy used for the sake of checking off a list of strategies sounds more like compliance and less like purposeful, engaged ownership. When students own their reading, they are decision makers, active participants, and highly motivated.

Let's take a look at how Gail took on very different roles with her students. First, Gail told the students what she had been noticing about their reading. She showed students examples and did not judge them, just offered them as examples, creating a space where students see there is not just one way to do something as a reader. She served as a mirror to the class. Next, Gail showed authentically what she does as a reader. She was a model and approached her students as a fellow reader, not an assigner. She is someone who reads and makes authentic choices. Then, Gail mentored students about the choices they wanted to make about their reading time. She did not assign a task, nor did she just say, "Go find something to do." She offered choices and mentioned when she thought they might be most useful. During the independent reading time, Gail did not monitor and correct. She uncovered what students were doing, how they were doing it, and why they were doing it. She was like a miner, trying to find helpful nuggets, assessing what students were doing. Finally, Gail was a facilitator of choices, not a manager of them. Gail offered ways the readers in the class might want to find closure in the period, and students self-selected what they needed. Gail's students made choices about how they would use their reading time, how they read, what they talked about in conferences, how they wrote about their thinking, and how they talked about their reading. Choice was embedded in each part of the reading period.

Students self-select the tools they need during independent reading. They have ownership of what and how they read.

Gravity Goldberg

Taking on New Teacher Roles: The 4 Ms

The roles of assigner, monitor, and manager limit the student role to being compliant. If we want to see true ownership, we can shift our roles. In the rest of this book, I describe the four new roles as reading teachers that I believe we need to take on in order to transform our classrooms:

1. We can be a **miner**, uncovering what and how students read.

2. We can be a **mirror**, giving feedback that tells students what they already know how to do.

3. We can be a **model**, showing students what we do as readers.

4. We can be a **mentor**, guiding students toward new ways of reading that work for them.

The following chart shows how each role has a different area of focus, either assessment, feedback, demonstration, or guided practice.

Role	Description	Focus
Miner	Uncover what students do and think as readers.	Assessment
Mirror	Reflect back what you see and hear readers doing.	Feedback
Model	Show what you do as a reader.	Demonstration
Mentor	Guide the reader to try something new.	Guided practice and coaching

Teachers' Roles When Fostering Ownership

Students' Roles

Once we shift our roles as teachers, students are positioned differently in the classroom. They are no longer left to complete our assignments, prove they did the assignments well, and follow our directions. In classrooms where students own their own reading lives, they are operating with a full sense of agency. They make choices, reflect on those choices, and are decision makers. These students tend to have the following characteristics:

- They care deeply.
- They set goals, intentions, and purposes for reading.
- They transfer reading strategies from one context to the next.
- They make informed choices.
- They question, critique, and problem solve.
- They initiate.
- They reflect.
- They know what works for them.
- They know not just what they like to read, but how they tend to read.
- They talk about their reading with passion and authenticity.
- They use writing as a tool, when needed, for making meaning.
- They choose the strategies they need when they need them.
- They read by choice.
- They identify as readers.

Of course, this list is not a static set of behaviors, but surely characteristics to strive for as we teach students in ways that support this new sense of agency.

How Ownership Sits Within the Gradual Release Model

It is likely that no classroom is either teacher or student owned. Instead, there is a day-to-day continuum that exists where students and teachers share the ownership. Or, in many cases, it may be that for certain parts of the reading period, the teacher takes on a behavior—say, assigning a task—but the students are expected to self-monitor their work. For the teacher, this ebb and flow of ownership is borne out of both reflection and careful planning, and the "learned intuition" and spontaneous decision making that experienced teachers do as they respond to students, moment to moment.

For example, Gail spent time honestly looking at her reading classroom and thinking about where she and her students tended to fall on the continuum. She reflected on the gradual release model of instruction, which calls upon students to take on more and more responsibility over time, and then she deliberately made changes so that she gave her students significantly more time to practice, to own the work of learning.

Mostly Teacher's Responsibility	Shared Responsibility	Mostly Students' Responsibility
Read to	Read with	By their side
I go	We go	You go
Interactive Read Aloud	Shared Reading	Reading Workshop

How Student Responsibility Sits Within a Balanced Literacy Model

In classrooms that use the gradual release model, the teachers take on more of the responsibility by modeling first, then inviting students to join them, and finally releasing the reading to the students to do on their own. I tend to simplify it by explaining to students, "I go, then we go, then you go" (see the chart above and Appendix C). In classrooms that use a balanced literacy framework, there are components that correspond to the continuum of responsibility (see Appendix B as well as the ownership continuum earlier in this chapter). The most amount of teacher support where students have the least amount of responsibility is the Interactive Read Aloud. Teachers read the text aloud and model their reading and thinking. When the teachers read with students in Shared Reading, a text is enlarged so that everyone can read it together, discuss it, and share the responsibility of making meaning. Students take the lead during Reading Workshop where they direct their own reading and the teacher is by their sides, supporting them in conferences and small groups while also leaving large chunks of time for students to read on their own.

In his groundbreaking book *Choice Words*, Peter Johnston (2004) explains why we as teachers can't take on all of the responsibility and the importance of helping students develop agency. He explains,

> Developing in children a sense of agency is not an educational frill or some mushy-headed liberal idea. Children who doubt their competence set low goals and choose easy tasks, and they plan poorly . . . Children with strong beliefs in their own agency work harder, focus their attention better, are more interested in their studies, and are less likely to give up when they encounter difficulties than children with a weaker sense of agency (Skinner, Zimmer-Gembeck, & Connell, 1998). Feeling competent, these children plan well, choose

challenging tasks, and set higher goals. Their concentration actually improves when they face difficulties, and in the process of engaging difficulties they learn more skills. (Johnston, 2004, p. 40)

When we gradually release responsibility to students and mentor them in making choices, they can begin to increase their confidence and their sense of agency. This agency helps students move into greater independence and ownership.

In many classrooms, this focus on the gradual release model seems to be stuck in second gear. There are parts of the model operating, but common pitfalls prevent it from helping readers fully develop their ownership and understanding. The chart on the next two pages illustrates some common pitfalls that may happen when we attempt to implement a gradual release model in reading classrooms and then offers ideas for what the lesson could be. For example, for many of us, our demonstrations are meant to be short so students have time to go off and read on their own, but we may end up taking too much time, leaving students to passively watch us eat away their reading time. Another example is when we turn our guided practice experiences with "turn and talks" to a partner into a quick round of "fill in the correct answer" or "guess the teacher's thinking." We want students to have time working together but may end up doing so much of the work that we lead them to answer our closed-ended questions—those with a "right answer." And we may be so tense about time that we don't give students sufficient time to do the vital, messy work of developing ideas together.

Johnston (2004) explains, "No learner can afford to be dependent on the teacher for everything that needs to be noticed, so teachers have to teach children to look for possibilities" (p. 17). When teachers shift their roles away from managing, assigning, and monitoring, more space is created for students. In that space, there is room for possibilities. Both the teacher and the student can co-create, collaborate, and share the responsibilities of being readers. These relationships become dynamic as *students* begin to manage, assign, and monitor their own reading.

There is more to seeing these possibilities, though. What we see depends on what we are looking for, and what we are looking for depends on the lens we use to view our students. When we use a deficit lens, we look for what students do not know how to do. An admiring lens means we look for what students already know how to do, and instead of seeing problems, we see potential.

I Go: Demonstrations	We Go: Guided Practice	You Go: Independence
Description: Teacher demonstrates a strategy. This can take the form of think-alouds while reading during minilessons and read alouds.	**Description:** Teacher and students work together in a shared reading experience. Students work in pairs and small groups practicing the strategy that was modeled by the teacher.	**Description:** Students independently read and apply strategies as needed.
Common Pitfalls: The teacher demonstrates for half an hour while students sit passively and watch.	**Common Pitfalls:** During turn and talks, the dialogue is superficial and doesn't move students any closer to independence.	**Common Pitfalls:** Students mimic what the teacher just taught and don't choose when a strategy applies.
What It Could Be: • Break down strategies into smaller lessons and keep each demonstration shorter. We don't have to demonstrate all we know in one lesson. • Give students a focus for what to watch for while you demonstrate.	**What It Could Be:** • Use turn and talks for open-ended and purposeful practice. • Teach students how to talk well and what makes an effective discussion. • Less can be more. Offer students a bit longer to talk and have fewer turns.	**What It Could Be:** • Mentor students in how to make choices. Show them how you decide what strategies to use when. Then give them permission to do the same. • End minilessons with a brief moment to review an anchor chart and past strategies and then ask students to set an intention to guide their choices.

(Continued)

(Continued)

I Go: Demonstrations	We Go: Guided Practice	You Go: Independence
Common Pitfalls:	**Common Pitfalls:**	**Common Pitfalls:**
The teacher models a strategy that isn't relevant at that juncture for many readers.	During shared reading experiences, the teacher still does most of the work and asks students to guess her correct thinking.	When students struggle, they sit and wait for the teacher to come solve the problem.
What It Could Be:	**What It Could Be:**	**What It Could Be:**
• Use ongoing formative assessment and conferences to plan what strategy will be modeled for students. What do many of them need to learn right now? • Make sure your curriculum doesn't box you in too much. Privilege what you know students need over what a document says.	• Plan what questions you will ask and where in the text you will ask them ahead of time. Make sure they are open-ended and authentic so students can practice strategies (not answer right/wrong questions). • Sit with students and not in front of them so you can physically be reminded you are sharing the work with them.	• Have charts and other reminders for students that they can refer to when they feel stuck. • When students struggle, show them you believe in them by asking, "What could you try to solve that problem?" • Frame challenges as opportunities to learn and grow. Celebrate how students approached problems on their own.

The Gradual Release Model: Stuck in Second Gear

What's Next?

This book looks at how we position ourselves as teachers and the ways it can lead to student ownership. For the sake of simplicity, I distilled these stances into four roles, and in this book, you will learn how to be miners, mirrors, models, and mentors to readers along with the behaviors and actions that characterize these roles.

When teachers shift their roles, there is space for students to begin reading with a sense of agency, making choices and initiating purposeful reading experiences. Having worked with teachers who are like Gail, I know reader ownership is possible, especially if you approach students with an admiring lens.

In **Chapter Three,** I more clearly describe what admiring readers means and why it is so vital in creating ownership. Then, in the following chapters, I break down how to go about creating classrooms where students don't just read on their own but also own their reading.

Chapter Four focuses on showing what classrooms look like when space is created for ownership. We step into classrooms and look at photographs of meeting areas, reading nooks, classroom charts, and student work.

Chapters Five through Eight each focus on one of the teacher roles. Each of these 4 *M* chapters describes step-by-step how you can take on the role of miner, mirror, model, and mentor.

Chapter Nine offers specific lessons you can teach the readers in your classroom. These lessons focus on teaching readers how to talk about their reading process, set goals, reflect on their mindset, give feedback, and ask for support.

Chapter Ten leaves you with a few entry points for getting started as admirers. I offer ideas for where and how you might begin taking on these new roles and setting students up to truly own their reading lives.

CHAPTER THREE

Being an Admirer

Looking at Readers
With Curiosity

Andrew Levine Photography

In the previous chapter, I talked about shifting roles for teachers and students so that students could take on greater independence as readers, and the 4 *M*s of being a miner, a mirror, a model, and a mentor. Now, let's look more deeply at how we can change our relationships with our students so that these new roles can occur. The very first step is to learn to *admire* the readers with whom we work. Let me explain what I mean by that word.

I spend most of my time studying and researching readers—getting to know them as people, as thinkers, as idea makers, and as problem solvers. To study something or someone closely is really an act of admiration. To admire means to regard with wonder and surprise. Lucy Calkins, one of my mentors, said that skillful teaching of reading is an art (2001), and ever since then, I have seen it through that lens. The artists I know are also admirers, looking at the world with wonder and awe. Our country's focus on science, technology, engineering, and math (STEM) has evolved to include the arts (STEAM). We want our students to have the investigative and innovative dispositions of scientists but also the creativity of artists. Therefore, we cannot simply collect data and reduce our students to numbers, levels, and charts. If we want to cultivate environments where students thrive, we can practice the same traits that scientists and artists practice—we can admire our students. I mean not just to respect them, but to approach them with wonder and curiosity—to study our students with the expectation they have many things to teach us.

Author Katherine Bomer talks about the power of looking for what student writers are already doing and about honoring that in her book, *Hidden Gems: Naming and Teaching From the Brilliance of Every Student's Writing* (2010). She explains, "My hope is that as teachers we can respond to all students' writing with astonished, appreciative, awestruck eyes" (p. 7). When we respond in this way, we are carrying an admiring lens into our work with students and seeing the gems they have to offer.

Admiring Allows Us to See What Is There

I'm challenging us to view readers differently—with promise, expectation, and admiration. Doing so requires us to build a different sort of relationship with our students. Rather than approaching students through a deficit lens, looking for what they are not doing or doing wrong, we can approach them with admiration—through an admiring lens. When students are approached from a deficit lens, they are often labeled, fixed, or discounted (Flores, Cousin, & Diaz, 1991; Goldberg, 2014). Hattie (2012) explains deficit thinking this way: "We invent so many ways in which to explain why students cannot learn; it is their learning styles; it is right or left brain strengths or deficits; it is lack of attention . . . it is lack of motivation . . . because they do not do their work" (p. 25). He explains that, when we look at students with a deficit lens, we explain away why achievement is not happening, and we place the emphasis on what we cannot control. On the contrary, he found what did help student achievement was when teachers realized "that teachers' beliefs and commitments are the greatest influence on student achievement over which we can have some control" (Hattie, 2012, p. 25). If we look at what students are doing, we are admiring who the reader is. We can look at students' process and their approximations as signs of growth, worthy of our wonder and curiosity.

I found myself underlining Hattie's words about teachers' beliefs and commitments being an area *over which we can have some control* because it's so true; there is so much we can't control, from students' parental involvement to their tastes in books, so why not make the best use of our power, by being much more mindful of our actions and intentions as reading teachers?

Shawn Achor, a positive psychologist out of Harvard University and author of *The Happiness Advantage: The Seven Principles of Positive Psychology That Fuel Success and Performance at Work* (2010), describes what happens when we focus on what is wrong instead of what is right. He explains how a group of tax auditors at a Fortune 500 company admitted to suffering from depression and family issues. One man confessed that he had spent the past few weeks noticing all of his wife's mistakes and created a spreadsheet of them so she could perform better in the future. Luckily the man shared this list with Achor before showing it to his wife, and was convinced this would likely not go over well at home.

While it can be easy to laugh at the ridiculousness of this man's actions, Achor studied why this happened. He realized that the main function of these tax auditors' jobs was to look for and find mistakes. They literally looked at documents all day long trying to find errors. This created the patterning and habit of looking for mistakes and errors everywhere, not just at work. They could not simply turn this mindset off when the workday ended. As a result, they were miserable at work and at home. Achor taught them to change their habits so they could change their mindset. Instead of looking for mistakes all day long, they looked for what is correct and then noticed the few times when documents had errors. Rather than thinking, "Mistake, mistake, mistake," they changed their habits to think, "Correct, correct, correct, and this one is a mistake, correct, correct . . ." By putting their attention on what was correct, most of the time they were still able to find errors and keep their jobs, but they were much happier employees and people. Achor (2010) explains, "Constantly scanning the world for the negative comes with a great cost. It undercuts our creativity, raises our stress levels, and lowers our motivation and ability to accomplish goals" (p. 91). An admiring lens can help us notice what is already going well for readers. It can also help us stay creative and motivated and be less stressed.

Seeing What Is There

Derek was a third grader in an inclusive classroom. Almost every day, he missed out on most of the time set aside for partner conversations at the end of Reading Workshop. Like the rest of his classmates, Derek had a plastic bag filled with self-selected books that he chose every week or so. Somehow, it seemed like his bag of books always went missing when it was time to discuss his thinking with his partner. While it would have been easy for me to reprimand Derek and punish him for wasting time because he was not organized, I chose to use an admiring lens instead.

I spent a minute or two each day watching Derek at the end of independent reading time when it came time to gather or put away his books and transition to partner time. Rather than thinking about what he was not doing, I focused on what he was doing. I noticed Derek was lining up his books in size order from the smallest to largest widths and then carefully putting each book in the plastic bag one at a time. This took him twice as long as it took the rest of the students in the class. Then Derek seemed to notice the rest of the students had already gathered with their partners to discuss their reading and thinking. At this point, Derek seemed frantic to catch up to the others and begin talking with his partner. This meant he either dropped his book bag, forgot to bring the books, or rushed over to find his partner, often tripping over a classmate or disrupting the other readers who had already begun talking.

By looking for what was there, I noticed a few traits that Derek did have that I had previously missed.

- Derek chooses books he wants to read.
- Derek cares for and organizes his books carefully.
- Derek wants to talk with a partner and is upset when he misses out on some of the discussion time.

While Derek could benefit from learning ways to organize his books that would be more time efficient, I learned so much about Derek from admiring what he already did as a reader that could be built upon.

Admiring Gives Us Glimpses
Into Our Students' Minds

The word *admire* comes from the Latin word *admirari*, which is *ad-* + *mirari*, which means "to wonder at." Admiring as it is used in this book does not just mean to want to be like another person. Admiration is not emulation. Every reader deserves to be seen and to be wondered about—as worthy of close study—not close study with the purpose of trying to correct, fix, or change the reader, but close study to figure out the complicated and beautiful ways this reader thinks and works. We cannot teach readers if we have not first admired them and fully wondered about who they are and how and why they read—what makes them the readers they are. One of Hattie's (2012) signposts for excellent teaching is the need for teachers "to be aware of what each and every student in their class is thinking and what they know" (p. 22). If you are admiring the readers in your class, you do know what is going on in their minds because you spend your time figuring out how the readers in your class read, not just what they read.

A reading conference is a great place to peek into a reader's mind and get to know him well. I can admire what he already knows how to do. This insight helps him build on strengths as we talk about next steps.

Wendy Murray

Peeking Inside a Student's Mind

I sat down next to Tiffany, an eighth grader who had been gripped by the *Twilight* book series written by Stephenie Meyer. When I approached Tiffany, she was so engrossed in the book she didn't even realize I was squatting next to her. After interrupting her reading, I began talking to her about why she was reading these books. Tiffany explained that she had already read this series and was on her second reading of the second book in the series. I wondered if this was the best use of Tiffany's independent reading time and what she was getting out of rereading these books that I judged to be rather poorly written.

Instead of putting my judgments about the books out there, I began to admire Tiffany and asked questions about her purpose and process of reading. I wanted to get a glimpse into her reading mind. Tiffany explained that she loved these books so much, and they were the first ones since she was a little kid that she really enjoyed reading. I asked her why, and she spoke about feeling connected to the emotions and conflicts that the main character Bella experienced. This was surprising to me since Bella was struggling with how to date a vampire (not something I thought Tiffany was struggling with).

By asking lots of questions to try to uncover what exactly Tiffany was doing as a reader, I began to ask, "What are you thinking about?" and "How are you reading this differently this time than the first time you read it?" In this discussion, Tiffany revealed a bit about how her reading mind works by explaining she viewed Edward being a vampire as a metaphor and not just a made-up type of creature. She viewed Bella's struggles on a symbolic level—should she follow her attraction toward a boy who could take so much from her?

If I had written off Tiffany's choice to reread the *Twilight* series, I would have missed the opportunity to admire and really see how she read. I found out that Tiffany was a reader who could understand symbols and read metaphorically. By talking about how she read and not just what she read, I had a much better understanding and appreciation for this reader.

Dorothy Barnhouse and Vicki Vinton, authors of *What Readers Really Do* (2012), explain how they teach students to use a T-chart that has two columns, "What We Know" and "What We Wonder," as a simple tool to help make students' reading processes more visible. It is a tool they value because it "allows students to see the invisible process of their reading: how attending to details helps readers forge through confusion to draft and revise meaning" (Barnhouse & Vinton, 2012, p. 65). They often use read aloud experiences to discuss this invisible process where both the teacher and students discuss their process for making meaning. They do this because they value parts of reading like "inferring, understanding, and evaluating, that often remain invisible, in a supportive social setting" like read alouds (Barnhouse & Vinton, 2012, p. 67).

In their book *No More Independent Reading Without Support* (2013), Debbie Miller and Barbara Moss discuss why students need time to talk about what they read. Their research analysis shows that, when students are given time to talk to the teacher and to other students about their reading, they comprehend texts with greater depth. These conversations can also offer us a glimpse into the minds of readers to show us how they think about and construct meaning. Looking at how they construct meaning helps us see inside their reading minds.

Admiring Lets Us See Potential

Sir Ken Robinson's TED Talk and book *The Element* (2009, with Lou Aronica) claim that schools must shift to help connect students with their talents and passions. He explains that schools tend to narrowly focus on a small set of skills and only a few ways of demonstrating them. This means many students do not fit within these margins and, therefore, get labeled with a deficit lens. His book is filled with stories of now famous and successful people who performed very poorly in school. He claims that a major factor in people's later success was simply one adult who looked at these poorly performing students differently—as people with assets and with potential. In other words, they needed more teachers looking at them with an admiring lens. Mick Fleetwood, the drummer and cofounder of the band Fleetwood Mac, explains, "I was starting to get markers that it was okay to be who I was and to do what I was doing" (quoted in Robinson & Aronica, 2009, p. 29). He later went on to form one of the most influential music bands of his time. His teacher looked at him with wonder and acknowledged what he already did well that he could build upon.

Seeing Potential

During an interactive read aloud of the book *Naked Mole Rat Gets Dressed* (2009) by Mo Willems, a group of fifth-grade readers discussed lessons they learned from the book. The book is about a mole rat named Wilbur who likes to wear clothes, something that is just not done in his community. By being true to himself, his decision to wear clothes pushes his fellow mole rats to consider if they need to be more open to differences. Students jotted down their thinking as we read the book and then discussed their ideas in a whole class conversation. The students ran the conversation as I listened and scribed the ideas they stated on a whiteboard.

Most of the readers judged the mole rats as closed-minded and came down quite harshly on their decision to ostracize Wilbur for wearing clothes and being different. One reader, Jessica, was more sympathetic to the mole rats, inferring what was driving their actions. She explained, "The naked mole rats judged Wilbur for wearing clothes without trying it themselves. It was hard for them to break what they were used to. They always had this stereotype about what naked mole rats were. But it is good to be quirky. That's what makes you you." After Jessica's comments, most of the readers in the class added evidence and ideas to support her thinking. Still, the readers seemed to be very focused on what the naked mole rats were not doing.

Then one reader brought a different lens to the conversation by focusing on the naked mole rats' potential. He explained, "By simply trying something new, you can decide for yourself if you like it. You don't need to limit yourself by saying you shouldn't do something until you actually try it." A few readers nodded after he spoke. The class spent the next few minutes discussing how not limiting yourself and seeing the potential of what could be helps you figure out who you really are.

We wrapped up the conversation by connecting the students to the lessons they had learned from the naked mole rats. Where did they limit themselves, and where did they see potential for who they could be as readers? The students spent the final three minutes reflecting on and writing about these questions.

When we focus on possibility instead of limitations, we have space to be who we are and move toward who we want to become as readers and as people. When we let an admiring tone settle in to our every moment, students feel safe enough to risk-take with their ideas about books and life.

In classrooms where there are daily times for discussion, students learn to share their individual interpretations along with how to listen and learn from one another. Readers can work together in a conversation to better understand a text and themselves.

Gravity Goldberg

Admiring Helps Us Recognize Individuality

As a child, I had a rock collection. I did not set aside time to go find rocks, but instead the rocks seemed to find me. If I was on a hike, I would get a glimpse of something shiny and stop to go find a piece of mica glittering from the corner of a larger black rock. I would pick it up and place it in my pocket. While riding my bike with friends, I would stop to check out the big rock my wheel rode over. This rock would end up in the bike's basket and, ultimately, in my collection. I would sit with my box of rocks and study each one carefully. I was around five years old, so I did not know the fancy words for what I was looking at. Rather than sort the rocks by labels that someone else had told me, such as sedimentary or igneous (which were far beyond my vocabulary), I sorted them by the characteristics I noticed. My dad helped me build my own rock display case out of a box and cardboard. When family or friends looked at my collection, I would ask, "What do you notice about this rock?" pointing to one. I wondered if they noticed the same things I did. Or I would ask, "Guess what I love about this rock?" To me, each rock was beautiful, perfect, and worthy of close study. I admired each rock.

Seeing Individuality

I sat with three readers, Don, Marilee, and Hung, for a small group reading lesson. I called these three readers over to meet with me because they were all on the same reading level and I wanted to help support them moving to another level. They tended to have success independently reading and understanding books that were at levels H and I, but when attempting to read level J books, they encountered many challenges.

I introduced the *Mr. Putter & Tabby* series to them—showing the books and explaining a bit about the characters and why I enjoyed them so much. I invited the students to read one of the books. Each student chose a title and previewed the book's cover and pictures. One by one, the students began reading the books they had chosen. I took this opportunity to be a miner and began to uncover what they were doing as readers in this new level book.

I noticed that Don read every word easily and fluently and zipped through the pages quickly, barely looking at the pictures. Marilee looked at the illustrations on each page carefully before attempting to read the words on each page. Hung laughed and pointed to funny parts as he read. He muttered to himself, "Mr. Putter is like a little boy." By admiring each reader's process, I was able to see who each one was in this moment as a reader.

Even though these students are at approximately the same independent reading level, they are very different readers with individual ways of reading and enjoying books. Knowing this allows me to approach them in very different ways, honoring and building off of who they are and how they read.

Admiring Pushes Us to Be Precise

Peter Roget, known as the creator of the thesaurus, spent his life studying words. At age eight, he wrote his own book, which was a list of words translated from Latin to English. As he grew, he studied science and spent time wandering the garden and describing what he saw. He liked to find the precise words for things and kept lists of words by category. He pursued a higher education and became a

Being Precise

I sat with a team of second-grade teachers, looking at students' running records, written assessments, and the teachers' anecdotal conference notes. We were using this time to decide on next steps in instruction for readers who were studying characters. We looked at students' work and tried to name what they were doing and approximating. From there, we built a staircase, as shown, placing more sophisticated analysis on higher steps. Rather than simply saying students "got it" or "didn't get it," we tried to name more precisely what they were trying to do.

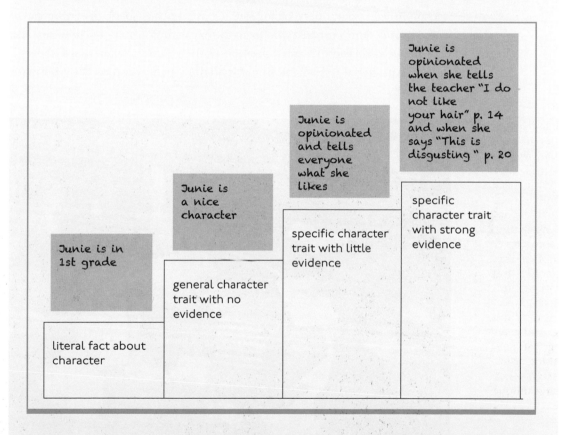

After we built the staircase, we placed students in groups and looked ahead at the next step to decide what we could model for them. This was not an activity about labeling students or grading them. Rather, it allowed us to specifically name what students did so we could precisely decide what we might teach them next.

doctor and a lecturer, but he never lost sight of his interest in words. He admired words for what they meant and how they could be used. He believed "everyone should be able to find the right word whenever they needed it" (Bryant & Sweet, 2014, p. 27). In 1852, when Roget published his first thesaurus, the book was a huge success. He chose to call the book *thesaurus* because the term means "treasure house" in Greek. This was the perfect name for a book of lists written by someone who admired words. When you admire someone or something, you do not settle for surface understandings; you seek precision.

Admiring Gives Us the Small and Big Picture

Accomplished evolutionary biologist E. O. Wilson has spent his entire career studying ants. One journalist who spent the day with Wilson noted how he walks with his head cocked in a tilted position (French, 2001). When asked about it, Wilson explained it was a habit from his lifetime spent scanning the ground for

Students work together in large groups as well as with partners. They are referring back to entries in their reading notebooks and explaining their thinking to one another. Peer discussions and peer work tap into the social aspect of reading and learning. And peers' language can help something "click" for a classmate in a way that is unique.

Gravity Goldberg

insects. French explains a moment observing Wilson admire ants: "As I caught up with him, intending to introduce myself, he stooped down low toward the garden's dirt path to pick one up, pronouncing its scientific name with the raw delight of a boy hobbyist, and exclaiming." As an admirer of ants, Wilson is considered the foremost expert on the insect. Later in his career, he began to see how the small creatures can teach us about larger issues and challenges across the planet. Admiring allows him to see the small and the big and to focus on both.

As reading teachers, let's spend our time admiring readers. This means we see differently, noticing what already is there. We also listen differently, getting glimpses into the readers' minds and process. As admirers, we find potential and imagine what could be. We get beyond surface understandings and find the precise ways readers work.

Seeing Big and Small

I projected a photo on the board and asked, "What do you notice?" This happened to be a photo that inspired my personal narrative about the moment before starting the swim portion of a triathlon. The picture showed a group of women in wetsuits and swim caps, staring into the water. The students took a few seconds to look at the photo and then turned to their partners and described what they saw—most of them listed objects and descriptions. "There are a bunch of people with black suits on and pink swim caps," or "There is a blue arch and people."

My colleague, Michael, stood up on a chair, extended his arms wide, and told the students to imagine he was an eagle. As an eagle, he could soar high into the air and look down at everyone and everything. He could see the big picture, the forest, the colors, but not the tiny details. "When we look at the world in big-picture ways, we are using our Eagle Vision," I explained. "When you looked at this photo, most of you glanced at it quickly, took in the whole of it, and noticed the bigger parts up front first." Students nodded their heads.

(Continued)

(Continued)

Michael drew his hands in close, squatted down, and pretended he was a mouse. He asked the students to notice how a mouse can only see the small little things around him. A mouse would not even miss a crumb on the ground because that would be dinner. A mouse lives close to the ground and cannot take in the big picture; he can take in only the little details around him.

I asked the students to look back at this photo with Mouse Vision and to jot down what they saw. Then each student shared his or her observations with a partner. The room began to buzz. The students noticed so much more. "They are barefoot, and some have these black straps on their ankles." "There are people swimming in the lake, and wakes are moving from them. Oh, and there are people in kayaks in the water." They had so much to say and seemed to notice many details.

"When we read, when we write, and when we live our lives," I explained, "we have choices to make. Are we going to use our Eagle or our Mouse Vision? When we choose to be eagles, we see the whole, the big picture, but we might miss the little, interesting details. When we choose to be mice, we see up close, so we don't miss any little things, but we might not see how all those little things fit together." I wanted the students to know that how we view the world affects the meaning and experiences we make. The beauty is that both eagles and mice are perfectly wonderful as they are. We don't need to change anything. But as people, we can learn from both of them, not overvaluing one way of being over the other, instead intentionally choosing how we want to interact with our texts, our readers, and our worlds.

Admiring Supports a Growth Mindset

Part of our role as admirers is to figure out the type of mindset students hold about themselves as readers. This concept of mindset comes from Carol Dweck's (2007) research on growth mindset, which dramatically shifts the ways we think about intelligence and motivation. Dweck is the author of the book *Mindset: The New Psychology of Success* (2006). She is a psychologist and professor at Stanford University. After several large-scale studies, she and her colleagues found that students tend to have either a fixed or a growth mindset about ability.

Students with fixed mindsets explain ability as something you have or do not have. You are either good at reading or not. There is little you can do to change the ability. Students with fixed mindsets can be high or low achieving, but they tend to have common characteristics. Dweck (2007) explains, "Students with a fixed mindset become excessively concerned with how smart they are, seeking tasks that will prove their intelligence and avoiding ones that might not. The desire to learn takes a backseat." The startling results of several studies show that students with fixed mindsets tend to care most about whether others judge them as smart or not. They also tend to avoid opportunities to take risks or try something that may lead to a mistake. If a mistake is made, they tend to try to hide it and often show little ability to recover from setbacks (Dweck, 2007). One detrimental belief that students with fixed mindsets tend to hold is a fear of effort. They equate effort with ability and think that effort makes you look dumb. If you are good at something, you should not have to use effort (Blackwell, Trzesnewski, & Dweck, 2007).

In contrast, students with growth mindsets view ability as something someone can develop through effort and education. Students with a growth mindset actually enjoy challenge rather than eschew it. "When students believe that they can develop their intelligence, they focus on doing just that. Not worrying about how smart they will appear, they take on challenges and stick to them" (Dweck, 2007). Students with growth mindsets tend to care about learning and view effort as a positive trait. If they do make a mistake, they work harder and try to learn new strategies. It is not surprising that Dweck and her colleagues found that students with growth mindsets outperformed their peers with fixed mindsets because a growth mindset fosters the motivation and beliefs about growth over time.

Readers with fixed mindsets might think, "I am not a good reader, so I will do enough to get by." Or they might think, "I am a really good reader, but I am having trouble with this book, so I better hide my struggle and pretend I get it." A reader with a growth mindset might think, "I want to learn how to read more complex books, so I better spend more time reading." Or the reader might say, "I am working on trying to keep track of my thinking across a whole book, and I need some help with that. I keep trying different ways and think I need to find a new one that will work for me."

A big part of our role as admirers of readers is to focus not just on what readers do and think but on the beliefs and mindsets they carry with them. My hunch is that readers with a fixed mindset may tend to be compliant readers while readers with a growth mindset may tend to have a greater sense of agency and ownership. "A safe environment for the learner (and for the teacher) is an environment in which error is welcomed and fostered—because we learn so much from errors and from the feedback" (Hattie, 2012, p. 19). We can support students' growth mindsets by the way we frame struggle and mistakes in our classrooms.

The Duckworth Lab's research on grit is connected to the concept of growth mindset. The lab's research explains how deliberate practice, a part of having grit, is a marker of future success. "Deliberate practice is the sort of practice experts do to improve; it involves effortful striving toward a very specific goal whose level of difficulty exceeds current skill and demands feedback, most often, coaching" (Duckworth Lab, 2015). Those who hold a growth mindset tend to participate in deliberate practice and tend to view effort as a part of reaching their goals.

Blau (2003) explains the habits of mind of highly literate readers. These habits all include elements connected to growth mindset and grit. For example, one habit includes the willingness to take risks, and another includes tolerance for failure—a willingness to reread and reread again. The problem with using a fixed mindset with readers in schools is that, "when simple lack of appropriate effort is treated—as it often is—as a symptom of insufficient mastery of some sub-skill of reading, students are likely to be offered forms of instructional assistance that support inattention and confirm the student's own mistaken notion that they lack some specialized body of knowledge or reading skills that distinguish them from their teachers" (Blau, 2003, p. 19).

Admiring Creates Growth Mindset Expectations

Shawn Achor's (2010) research looks at the principles that fuel success and performance. He studies the connection between mindset, leadership, and happiness. One such study focused on how mood impacts the ability of the brain to process visual information. Researchers at the University of Toronto found that people who approached looking at an image with a positive mood saw more of the image than those who had a negative mood. Those who were positive actually expanded their peripheral vision to see more. In other words, if we approach readers with a negative lens, we may actually be missing some of what they are already doing.

Another study focused on what is called the Pygmalion Effect—how our expectations influence outcomes. Researchers found that second graders who were split into two groups, each with the same amount of teaching and prior knowledge, performed dramatically differently based on the expectations that were communicated by the teachers. Achor (2010) explains,

> Our belief in another person's potential brings that potential to life. Whether we are trying to uncover a talent in a class of second graders or in the workers sitting around the morning meeting, the Pygmalion Effect can happen anywhere. The expectations we have about our children, co-workers, and spouses—whether or not they are even voiced—can make that expectation a reality. (p. 84)

By approaching readers with an admiring lens, we are setting positive expectations for success.

Language Impacts Mindset

In *Opening Minds: Using Language to Change Lives* (2012), Peter Johnston explains how our language choices impact students' mindsets. When we praise the person rather than the process, we reinforce a static idea of ability. For example, when teachers praise students by giving feedback like "You are a good reader," the emphasis is on the person. This can create a fixed mindset about them as readers. If, on the other hand, process-oriented feedback is given, it reinforces a growth mindset. A teacher might say, "When you stopped to reread that confusing part, you were able to figure out what was going on. It really helped you understand the article." The process-oriented feedback puts the emphasis on the steps the reader took and shows the process has value.

We can also use students' language choices as windows into viewing their mindsets. When students talk about themselves as readers, we can begin to identify the type of mindset they hold. Johnston (2012) points out that when students say, "I've never been good at this sort of thing," or "I have a terrible memory," it shows a fixed mindset. This mindset can undermine motivation and effort, and alter the ways we experience ourselves as readers. We can teach students to hold growth mindsets by giving feedback and teaching them how to frame their struggles and process as a normal part of the learning process.

These three readers are members of a book club. They are all looking at one student's digital reading notebook and commenting on what she thought about and wrote about. They called me over to get feedback and admire their group's process.

Wendy Murray

Admiring Impacts Our Guiding Questions

Admirers study readers with guiding questions in mind. These questions frame what is seen. "What we see depends mainly on what we look for" (Sir John Lubbock, quoted in Rakestraw, 2012). When we use an admiring lens, we look for what readers are already doing and approximating. We also look for the type of mindset readers hold. In addition, we look for the readers' process—why, how, and what readers do. As reading teachers, we may keep one or more of these guiding questions in mind when we approach and study the readers in our classrooms, approaching them with curiosity and wonder.

You may want to compare the types of questions that guide your work with readers right now and consider replacing any of them that may contain a deficit lens. Consider the difference between this more deficit-minded guiding question—"Why can't Johnny identify themes?"—and this more asset-minded question—"What does Johnny already understand about theme?" We can also notice the difference between a product- and process-oriented set of questions. "What is the main idea of this article?" focuses on reading as a product and focuses on correct answers. "How do you go about reading nonfiction articles?" focuses on the process of reading and offers more insight into a reader's mind. The guiding questions in the following chart can be used with individuals, small groups, or an entire class of readers.

Focus for Admiring	Guiding Questions
Asset Lens	What is this reader already doing or approximating?
Mindset	What type of mindset is shaping this reader's experience right now?
Process	What, why, and how is this student reading? What is this reader's process right now?

Admiring Readers: Guiding Questions for Every Classroom Moment

Start Admiring!

While making changes and shifting your roles as a reading teacher, you have the opportunity to hold a growth mindset about your own ability as a teacher. Recall how people with growth mindsets practice deliberately, expect challenges, and realize that effort is a part of the learning process. Be kind to yourself and expect a bit of struggle. As you begin to admire the readers in your classes, see if you can also take on an admiring lens with yourself. What can you admire about your teaching? How can you see your own individuality, potential, and all that you already offer students? You can begin practicing admiration with yourself and then take this lens to your students.

In Chapter Four, I show you what classroom spaces look like when ownership and admiring are happening. This chapter takes you on a tour where we begin with the whole class instructional space; move to small group spaces, then to students' reading spaces; and end focusing on student work. The purpose of this chapter is to help you envision what these sorts of reading spaces look like. We can begin taking on new roles and using an admiring lens only when we can picture what this new way of being will be like.

CHAPTER FOUR

Creating Space for Ownership
A Photo Tour of Reading Classrooms

In this chapter, we take a step into classrooms where students already have ownership of their reading lives. I find it incredibly helpful to visualize what classrooms look like, sound like, and feel like when attempting to take on a shift in my own practice. There are several photos to examine and charts to study through the lens of admiring readers. Imagine this chapter as a tour where we begin with the whole class instructional space, move to small group spaces, and then move to students' reading spaces. We will end the tour by zooming in on student work. Each of these four stops along the tour will include photographs of physical space, resources, and student work along with my commentary. We are moving along the gradual release of responsibility model from more teacher modeling to shared experiences to independence. Let's take a walk.

Andrew Levine Photography

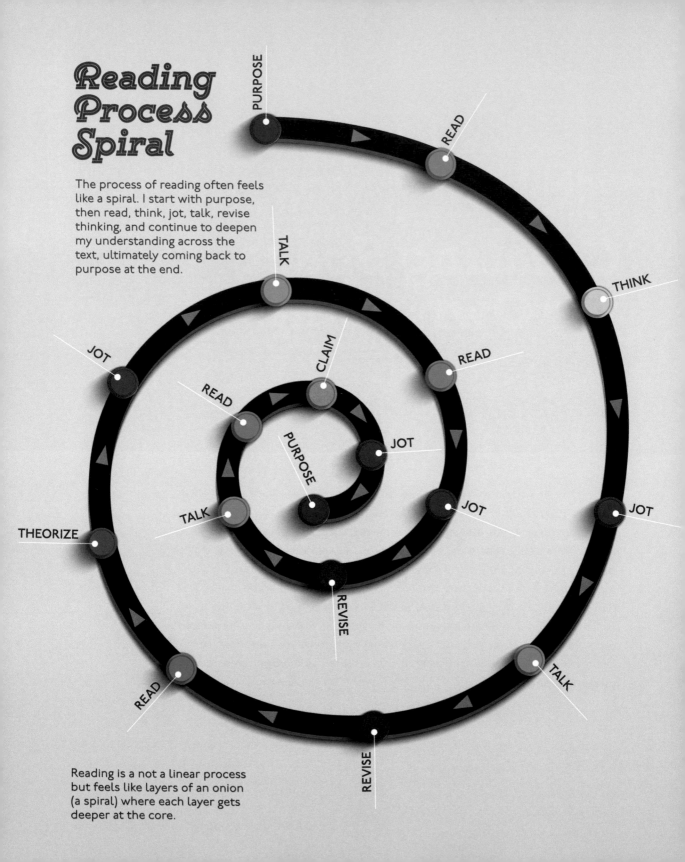

Reading Process Spiral

The process of reading often feels like a spiral. I start with purpose, then read, think, jot, talk, revise thinking, and continue to deepen my understanding across the text, ultimately coming back to purpose at the end.

PURPOSE

READ

THINK

TALK

JOT

CLAIM

READ

READ

JOT

PURPOSE

JOT

THEORIZE

TALK

JOT

REVISE

READ

REVISE

TALK

Reading is a not a linear process but feels like layers of an onion (a spiral) where each layer gets deeper at the core.

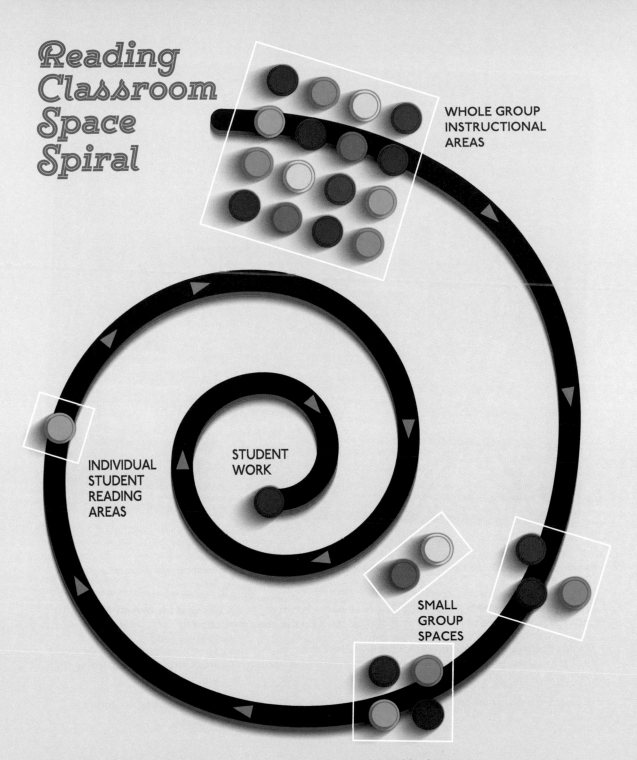

Reading Classroom Space Spiral

WHOLE GROUP INSTRUCTIONAL AREAS

INDIVIDUAL STUDENT READING AREAS

STUDENT WORK

SMALL GROUP SPACES

When I visualize what a Reading Workshop classroom space looks like, I see it as a spiral. There are layered spaces that serve different purposes—whole group instructional areas, small group spaces, and individual student reading areas—and at the core is the work students do.

Reading Workshop Space

Gravity Goldberg

Readers are spread out throughout the classroom and are engaged in independent reading and thinking.

The teacher meets with a student in the back of the room to review her goal for herself as a reader. Each student sets his or her own goal and places it on the class goal chart.

The teacher is able to take time to work with individual readers because the rest of the students are engaged in their reading experiences and are independent enough to work without interrupting their teacher.

The reader who is meeting with her teacher uses the goal to direct her own reading conference.

Class Meeting Area

Gravity Goldberg

Gail created a comfortable class meeting area so there would be space for modeling and shared experiences. By meeting together, the entire classroom community gathers to see demonstrations up close, discuss a read aloud book, or work together toward shared goals.

There is a handy basket of books that Gail loves and can use to model and show her reading process.

Gail includes a stool for a student to sit on up front and be a model too. Students, not just the teacher, have space to share what they do as readers.

An easel is front and center so Gail can model what she does as a reader and create collaborative charts with the students. The easel paper is empty because she shows her process in the moment in front of her students.

This is like a set for "Reading With Gail" where she has all her reading tools to be a model reader.

Meeting Area and Library

Pam Koutrakos

Pam's space is informal in nature and more like a space you would want to read in at home. There are cozy leaning pillows and a rocking chair.

Previously created charts are displayed by the meeting area so Pam and the readers can review them together. These charts help Pam mentor her students in making choices about how they will use their reading time.

The meeting area is surrounded by the classroom library. Simply by being surrounded by books, this area reminds students that there are hundreds of books to explore and enjoy.

Pam's library is organized in a few ways. The top shelf with the narrow yellow bins is for students' books and reading tools. Each student has his or her own reading bin, which contains books, a reading notebook, sticky notes, and writing pens. The blue bins of books are organized by theme, topic, or genre. The students participate in organizing books into these bins.

While many of the books in Pam's classroom library are leveled, the books are not organized by level. The levels are written inside the cover for those who need that support.

Students can organize books in ways that are engaging and authentic. In some schools, I have seen students label baskets of books as "Books That Are Now Movies," "Books That Will Make You Cry," "Adventure Books," and "Books You Will Want to Reread," in addition to genre-labeled baskets.

Reading Notebooks

Pam Koutrakos

Pam keeps her own reading notebook like her students. That way, she is not just telling students what she would do, but modeling what she is doing.

Pam personalized some of her reading notebooks and asks her students to do the same. This way, students have ownership of their notebooks and bring who they are into the reading classroom.

Reading notebooks are used as tools to deepen comprehension, not as assignments to prove to the teacher the students did the reading. Students choose when to write about a book and how to write about a book, and keep their purpose in mind as they read. This is all modeled by Pam first so students understand how to make these choices.

Gail Cordello

The students in Gail's classroom also personalize their reading notebooks. This information helps Gail know student interests and lets readers help each other find books on topics they care about.

By personalizing the notebooks, the students and teachers know these books belong to the reader and are not for the teacher.

Four main purposes for writing in the reading notebook are modeled so students can make choices about what they will write based on why they are writing. The four purposes include writing to clarify, writing to remember, writing to deepen thinking, and writing to prepare for conversations. Students choose how to write in relation to the purpose for why they are writing.

Reading Notebooks and Digital Notebooks

Gravity Goldberg

Students wrote about their thinking in their reading notebooks. Students chose the ways they wanted to document and keep track of their thinking.

Students reread their reading notebook entries and then formed claims they could support with evidence from the text. They formed their own claims based on what they learned from the novels they read.

Students wrote their own literary essays on Chromebook computers using Google Docs to collaborate and get feedback from their book club members.

Students shared their literary essays as well as their thinking processes with each other. Both the reading notebook and the digital notebook were used by students for different purposes. Students wrote about their thinking as they read in the reading notebook and wrote more formally for an outside audience in the digital notebook. They view the reading notebook audience as themselves and the digital notebook audience as other readers.

Laura Sarsten

In Laura's fourth-grade classroom, students are taught different ways they might choose to write about their reading. Using her own reading notebook, Laura models each one.

This chart shows how Laura mentors students in how to make choices about keeping track of their thinking. Students can then decide what will help them better understand particular books, and what works for them in general. Over time, students are introduced to more choices and invent their own ways.

Students wrote their choices and why they were making them on sticky notes. Then they added the sticky notes to the chart. These helped both Laura and the students recall their intentions.

Even though this choice chart is intended for students, it also helps Laura informally assess the types of choices students are making. She can reflect on the types of choices individuals and the entire class tend to make.

Student Examples From the Reading Notebook Choice Chart

> — Rules Book #4
>
> Today may goal is to start a chatacter timeline and a pastive and negitive chart. I am beggining my book so I want to learn about my character

> Today I am going to do a nemoraihal timeline. I am going to track Cathrine and how she acts to David and other characters. I will remember her down times and her up times. (Sad and happy.).

Laura Sarsten

These are two examples of students' choices about how they want to use their reading notebooks and the work they need to do as readers. Notice how each reader uses her own words to articulate what she is going to do and how she is going to do it.

These two students think not just about what choice they are making and how they are making it but also about why they are making this choice. Meghan is going to create a positive and negative chart to get to know the characters at the start of a new book. Nicolette is going to make a timeline so she can track the "down times and up times."

On any given day, students will be doing different types of writing about their reading based on who they are as readers, what their book requires of them, and their reading process. Students can track the types of writing they tend to do and how each one works for them. All of the choices are driven by purpose.

Student-Generated Challenge: Tracking Reading Volume

BOOKS READ DURING READING WORKSHOP

WHOLE CLASS READ ALOUDS

BOOKS READ FOR HOMEWORK

CLASS TOTALS BY MONTH

January 30th Exactly 1300 books!

Pam Koutrakos

Pam explained how this graph of monthly books read came from her students. "During a morning meeting, a member of our class said that the town's public library had this challenge to see how many books the town could read. It was a few hundred. I said, 'Well, we read so much in here, I bet we read more than the whole town!' The class jumped on it. A few volunteers went to talk to the librarians. Our class total blew theirs out of the water. However, then the class said we should continue to keep track and see if we could 'beat ourselves.' That's when we started tallying our reading approximately monthly."

By following her students' lead, Pam used her students' sense of competition to help them read more. They set the goal, and she helped them track it.

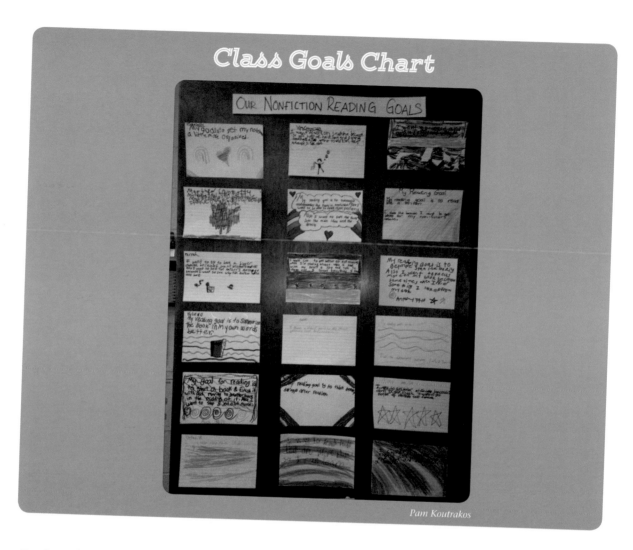

Class Goals Chart

Pam Koutrakos

Pam's reading curriculum is divided into units of study where the entire class reads a genre or studies a topic or theme. For example, the class has a unit of study where the students focus on characters, a unit of study on researching topics of interest, and a unit of study on how to read nonfiction. Toward the beginning of every unit of study, the students in Pam's class create personalized goals for themselves that go along with the theme or topic of the unit.

These goals are often developed with support from one another and their teacher, but the students ultimately create their own goals in their own words.

By displaying the goals, all the students in the class can help one another and remind one another about what they are working toward throughout the entire unit.

At the end of the unit, the readers can take these off the wall and reflect in writing or conversations about how they progressed and what they learned.

A little bit of color adds a lot of personalization to these goals and offers readers another vehicle for sharing their goals.

Student-Generated Research Topics

Informational Reading Topics

- CIA Torture Techniques, Fair/Unfair?
  *CIA torture techniques can be viewed as being both fair and
- Performance Enhancing Drugs & Athleth- Yes/No?
- Should the Penny be eliminated?
- Cell phone use in School Yes/No?
  *Cell phones in school can be both helpful and harmf
- Are school lunches healthy? Yes/No
- Should school start later? Yes/No
- Should colleges have access to your Social media profiles? Yes/No?
- Time Limits to Baseball Games Yes/No?
- Do Violent Video Games Make Kids More Violent Yes/No?
- Should we become vegetarians? Yes/No?
- Is D.A.R.E working in K-12? Yes/No?

Chris Fuller

In Chris's seventh-grade class, the students generated their own informational reading topics. The students chose what they wanted to study.

Chris's students met as a group and shared their topics as Chris listened and created this chart. The chart is also set up to connect to argument writing around these topics.

By being mentored to choose their own topics, the students were engaged and developed ownership of them. Because the topics were publicly displayed in the classroom, students began to form partnerships and small groups around similar topics on their own.

None of the students in this class forgot their articles or notebooks, and none asked, "How many articles do we have to read?" because they chose the topics and wanted to learn about them.

Book Club Tools and Spaces

Gail Cordello

Gail Cordello

The students in each book club in Gail's classroom are given a blue shallow bin to store their materials. Gail does not dole out materials or collect them. The readers are in charge of organizing and keeping track of their own tools.

Sometimes ownership is created by giving students tools that are theirs to use and organize.

A book club meets together at this small round table. Notice the teacher's chair is not here too. This is the student club members' space for reading, writing in their notebooks, and later discussing their interpretations of the book.

Even though these students are in the same book club and reading the same book, they take notes in their reading notebook in different ways. They choose how to track their own thinking.

Student Intentions

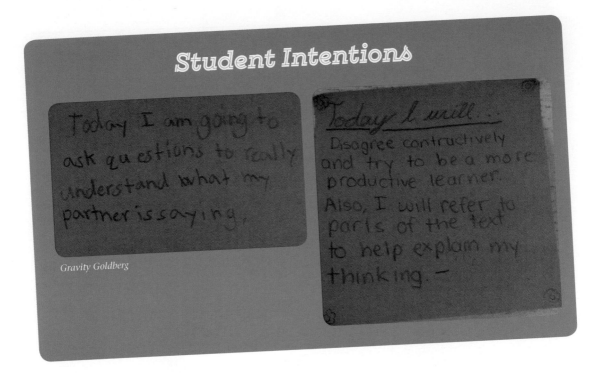

Today I am going to ask questions to really understand what my partner is saying.

Gravity Goldberg

Today I will...
Disagree contructively and try to be a more productive learner. Also, I will refer to parts of the text to help explain my thinking. —

Book club members Charlie and Olivia set intentions for themselves in terms of the conversational skills they want to work on.

These two readers are in the same book club but set different intentions for what they would like to work on during their club conversations.

Students' intentions often stem from what they have seen their teacher model, what other readers and clubs have modeled, and feedback from each other.

Small Group Instruction

Laura Sarsten

Laura calls a small group of readers over to a carpeted area of the classroom to model a strategy for them.

Notice how Laura is on the carpet with the students. She is at their eye level, talking to them as a reader herself.

Laura took notes prior to this lesson so she could offer the readers feedback. She referred back to these notes to give specific and growth mindset comments.

All of the students in this small group brought their books and reading notebooks with them so they could practice and apply what Laura was modeling for them in their own books.

These students read at different reading levels, and Laura is supporting them in a strategy she believes they all can benefit from learning. She is not teaching the content of a book but instead is teaching the readers a strategy. After modeling, she mentors them as they apply the strategy in their independent books. They begin transferring what she modeled in her book into their own books.

Reading Nooks

Laura Sarsten

These readers look focused, engaged, and comfortable independently reading. Just like adults, many students prefer to read in a cozy area and not at a desk.

These two readers are partners who meet daily for a few minutes after independent reading to discuss and check in. By sitting near one another, they can easily transition into a discussion by simply turning their bodies around.

These readers have all of their tools near them and set up their area each day to prepare to read.

When it comes time to have a discussion, they will simply turn and face one another. These students select their own topics for discussion and apply what their teacher modeled in terms of how to have productive conversations. They know how to listen actively, respond to clarify, and build on each other's ideas.

Gravity Goldberg

These four readers are all busy, focused, and working toward their goals.

Notice how each reader seems to be doing something a bit different based on what each one needs in the moment. One reader is stopping to jot a note in his notebook. Another reader is flipping back to a page in her book to reread an important part, while the others are moving forward in their books.

Gravity Goldberg

Readers in this classroom make choices. They choose what to read from the classroom library. They choose a place to read that will allow them to stay focused. They choose the tools that help them remember their thinking.

Notice one reader has her reading notebook out and another reader has a Chromebook computer and digital notebook out. They use these notebooks to write down and revisit their thinking. They often refer to these notebook entries when they have book club discussions with classmates.

Chart Supporting Independence

John Altieri

In John's second-grade classroom, he displays clear charts that students can refer back to while they read. He makes sure the charts are visible to all students while they read.

By using the exact words a reader might use when thinking about a text, he is offering a support that students can try out independently. He already modeled how he uses this language as a reader.

Over time, this chart might grow even more. Students can contribute other ideas for this chart and add what else they say to themselves as they read. For example, students might add phrases like "I am wondering about . . ." and "Now I know . . ."

Student-Organized Notebook

Laura Sarsten

Students' notebooks are a bit different because students made choices about what they look like and how they are organized.

By keeping a notebook and not worksheets for the teacher, the students develop ownership of the work they do as readers. A worksheet is for the teacher. A notebook is for the reader.

The teacher models different ways she tracks her thinking by showing T-charts, columns with categories, and timelines. By modeling strategies for tracking thinking in writing, she is setting her students up to be independent. When students are handed a worksheet or graphic organizer, they become dependent on us to give them tools in the future. Making their own graphic organizers in the notebook allows students to be more independent.

Notice how this reader used sticky notes to tab off the sections of her notebook. She also placed sticky notes on the front cover to remind her of what she chose to work on as a reader and book club member. Many of these notes include conversational phrases she wants to try when the club meets to talk.

Understanding Mindset Class Chart

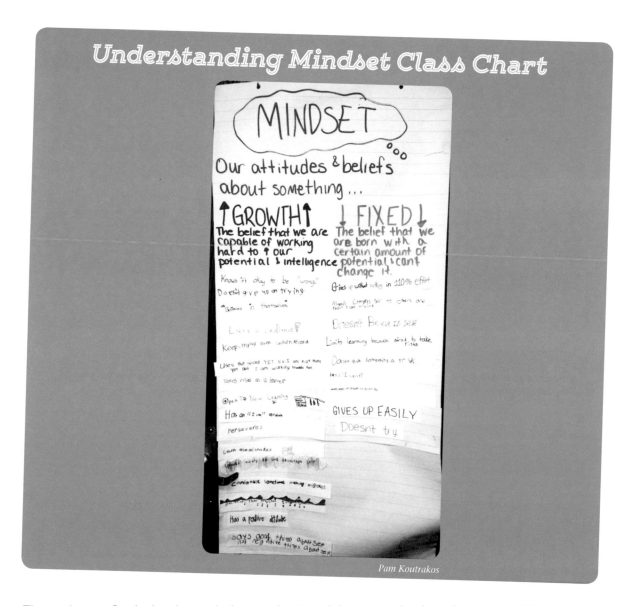

Pam Koutrakos

The students in Pam's class learned what mindset is and then created a class chart as an artifact they could refer back to throughout the year. By teaching what mindsets are, Pam helped the readers in this class to understand that they control their attitudes and beliefs.

Each student wrote an example of either a growth or fixed mindset belief or behavior. The class discussed each one, sorted the examples by type of mindset, and then glued them on the chart.

Readers in this class use this chart when setting goals, reflecting on their process, and giving feedback.

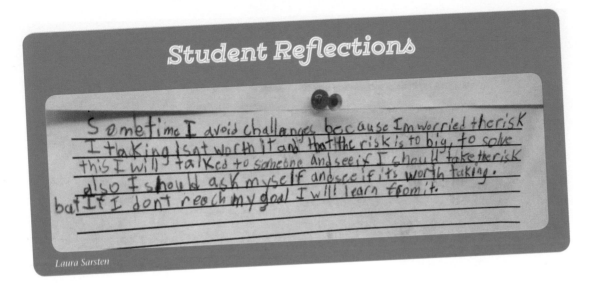

Student Reflections

Sometime I avoid challenges because Im worried the risk I taking Isnt worth it and that the risk is to big, to solve this I will talked to someone and see if I should take the risk also I should ask myself and see if its worth taking. but If I dont reach my goal I will learn from it.

Laura Sarsten

The students in Laura's class reflect on their reading process after talking as a class about the importance of taking risks and having a growth mindset.

Since these reflections are not for the teacher, but for the reader, students respond with honesty. They reflect across the year and notice how their mindsets change or develop across time.

7. Would you like to do this type of learning more often? If so, why?

I would like doing this type of learning. It's like choosing between working in an office or doing your dream job if you just try harder and put in more effort. The office builds a fixed mind and the dream job a social, hard-working, open mind.

Laura Sarsten

Reflection is built into the end of each unit of study, as in the case of this research reading unit. In this example, the teacher asks the students a few reflective questions to gather feedback about the impact of the learning from the students' perspective. The students, not just the teacher, have a say in assessing their learning.

This student wrote, "I would like to do this type of learning. It's like choosing between working in an office or doing your dream job if you just try harder and put in more effort. The office builds a fixed mind and the dream job a social, hard-working, open mind." This reader makes a connection between the jobs you take later in life and the type of mindset you carry.

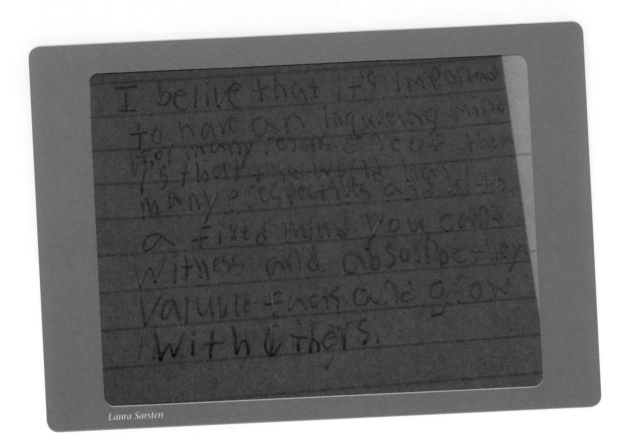

Laura Sarsten

Laura's students wrapped up their research and informational reading unit of study by discussing their beliefs about an inquiring mind. They wrote their beliefs on sticky notes, then participated in conversations with one another. They take time regularly to examine and discuss their beliefs.

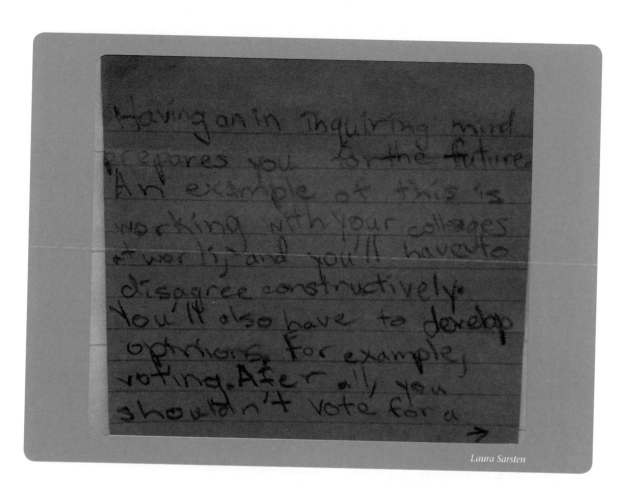

Laura Sarsten

The students often make connections to where and when the skills they are learning may help them later in life. They see the work they do as readers and thinkers as preparation for their future adult lives. Reading and reflecting are viewed as life skills and not just school tasks.

Reading Notebook Entries

Laura Sarsten

A — This reader chose how he wanted to set up his reading notebook and how he needed to write about the book and his thinking. He began by taking one of his sticky note ideas and then placed it at the top of his page to write longer about the idea.

B — Notice how he expands on his idea about the character and develops several interpretations of what is really going on in this part of the book.

C — The reader uses a visual of a web to list character traits. This reader knows that characters can have many sides to them and often display more than one trait.

D — The reader considers how the setting is impacting the character and how the choice the author made to include the number 13 could symbolize being unlucky.

E — In this one reading notebook entry, the reader demonstrates a deeper understanding of the book and how he is meeting many of the standards in this one entry.

F — Notice how this student's entry looks very different from his classmate's notebook (see the entry on the next page) even though they are reading the same book and in the same book club. These students have ownership of what they write down and how they write it.

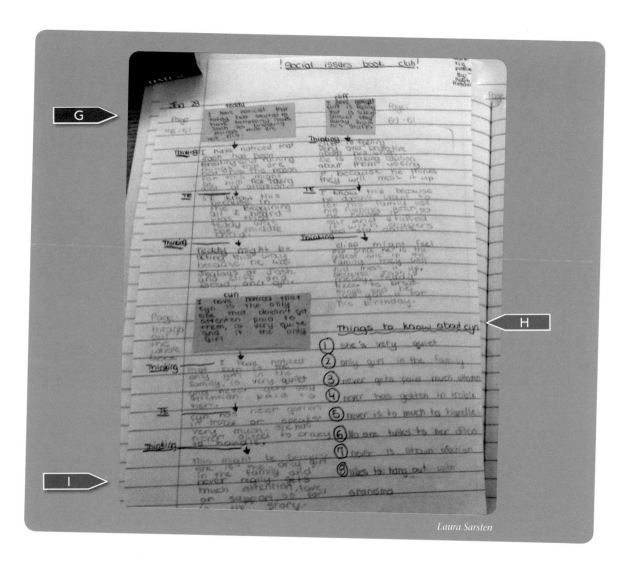

Laura Sarsten

G This reader set up her notebook to keep track of her thinking and the text evidence that supported it. Notice how she uses a combination of sticky notes, arrows to show the flow of her process, and labels to annotate her writing. She seems to have steps to her process: jot on a sticky note, write more about her thinking, and document the text evidence that supports it.

H After rereading these thinking and evidence entries, the reader synthesized the information and made a list of "things to know about" the character. This shows her thinking and writing process and allows her to draw conclusions about the character.

I The reader uses this list as conversational points to bring to her book club when it is time to have a discussion. She shows up prepared with ideas worth talking about.

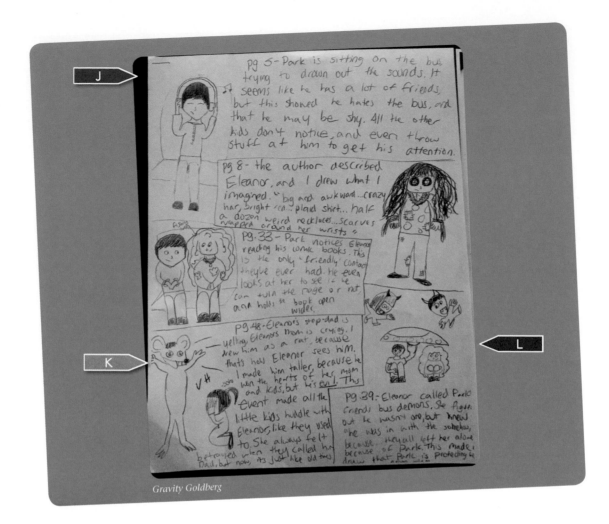

Gravity Goldberg

J — This seventh-grade student in an inclusive classroom chose how he wanted to track his thinking across an independent book. We can see he is visualizing the scenes, understanding literally what is happening, and also interpreting the character's motivation and reactions.

K — On the bottom left where the student drew the rat, he is considering symbols—the rat—and size to interpret power dynamics. The student is interpreting the character's feelings and experiences in the words next to the image.

L — The student's choice to organize his thinking in this way reveals much about how he thinks about books. From looking at this entry, I see he chooses important events (see page numbers and event summaries), visualizes (see the sketches with labels), interprets the relationships between characters (see his writing in most boxes), and bases his interpretations off of text details such as what characters say and do (see sketches and writing).

Conclusion

In this chapter, we took a tour into reading classrooms where students own their reading lives and teachers take on an admiring lens. If you are feeling inspired by what you have just seen (as I am), the remainder of the book will teach you how to create similar reading environments and readers in your classroom. In order to create classrooms where true ownership is happening, we teachers may need to take on different roles that encourage readers to do more, learn more, and read more. The next chapter focuses on how to take on the role of being a miner, uncovering your students' reading processes.

CHAPTER FIVE

Be a Miner
Uncovering Students' Reading Processes

MINER

MIRROR

MODEL

MENTOR

While at the beach last summer, I noticed a pair of young girls playing in the sand right near the water. I assumed they were about to make a sand castle and went back to reading my book. Then one girl shouted, "Come over here! I think we can find them here!" and I looked up, curious. The girl was waving her hands excitedly above her head, beckoning her friend. The second girl ran over, a bright-red shovel and pail in each hand. "Let's dig here, and I bet we find them!" the first girl exclaimed.

I put down my paperback. I watched.

Both girls were on their hands and knees. They dug with their fingers, and brought their faces close to the wet sand. They squinted. "Did you find one?" the second girl asked. "Not yet," the first girl replied. I noticed how intent they were on uncovering something from the sand. Shells? Sea glass? Were they young enough that they were pretending to find a pirate's treasure chest? I wondered. Digging their hands in deep was not working for them, and for some reason

Andrew Levine Photography

I admired that they didn't use their shovels—whatever they were after, they preferred the nimbleness and tactile sensation of their pearly little fingers.

One of the girls sat back on her knees and then scooched back to look at the scene from a bit farther away. I watched her gaze intently, her head shifting.

"Look," she said quietly to her friend, and just then I saw what she was noticing: small holes in the sand. "There are little dots here in the sand. I bet that's them."

The girls moved carefully around the dotted areas, and then, rather than digging deep into the sand, they began using the long edge of their small hands to gently sweep one layer of sand away at a time. They would sweep a bit, then look at each other and smile. Finally, one girl cheered, "I found one!"

I leaned forward to get a closer look, resisting the urge to jump up and go over to them. I wanted them to hold their finding up in the air so I could see it. But instead, the girls seemed to get still, and rather than pick it up, they kept sweeping the areas around the sand crab and created a sort of viewing gallery all around it. For several minutes they looked, pointed, and described what they saw. This crab had been uncovered and now was being admired by these two girls.

I learned so much from these young girls at the beach about what it means to be an admirer. They set an intention for what they hoped to look for, then looked closely for signs of where to find it, and purposefully uncovered layers that were keeping it hidden. They were miners, not seeking diamonds or gold, but seeking to see something new and rare. And once it was discovered, those girls didn't need to own it or control its movement in their red sand pail. Instead, they paused to see it, know it, and note its attributes.

As reading teachers, we need to do the same as those young girls. We need to pause to see it, to know it, and to note its attributes. We need to be miners, uncovering what students do as readers, getting into their reading minds, and uncovering layers of meaning that may often be hidden.

Using a Five-Step Process

What makes being a miner so difficult in reading is that most reading work is done in our minds and is invisible. There are no dots in the sand for us as markers. Our markers are often much harder to find because few reading behaviors are visible to us and the rest must be uncovered. It's not easy work—but it gets easier, and formative assessment is our best tool, for it's about trying to uncover what students already know and then using that information to plan future instruction. According to the International Literacy Association's Policy Brief (Snow & O'Connor, 2013), formative assessment is characterized by purpose, collaboration, its dynamic nature, and descriptive feedback.

In this chapter, we explore the ways in which mining is a form of formative assessment, and I share its five "steps" so that you can really understand how to do it. Mining goes beyond simply figuring out what readers know—it also includes figuring out *how* they know it. And as is true of all the 4 *M*s, mining is a mindset, too, a way of being with students that is an awful lot like the way those girls at the beach operated in their world of sand, ocean, and nature: focused, curious, determined, and admiring.

There are five main steps I take when being a miner of students' reading.

STEP 1: SET A PURPOSE

The first step I take as a miner is to set a clear purpose. I ask myself, *What am I mining for?* If I approach a student without a purpose, I tend to get overwhelmed and lost in what I am looking for. I could spend ten minutes or more with each student if I approached him with no purpose. I might end up listening to him read, then asking him to retell, then asking him to share interpretations, then getting him to explain the interpretations, as the minutes ticked by, and I still might be unclear on what he was doing, what I was really after, and as a result, my observations and notes would be diffuse. By contrast, when I set a clear purpose, I give myself permission to focus my observations and questions on one main area, and then I listen with that one focus in mind.

An important note: Each mining purpose is informed by the unit of study, curriculum, and standards, *but it is not necessarily the same for each reader in the classroom.* I may end up mining with different purposes in mind for different students based on who they are as readers and the types of texts they are holding in their hands. My first step is always to set a clear purpose for what I am mining for. The chart on the next page shows a few examples of mining purposes and how they may connect to an informational reading and research unit of study and the Common Core State Standards (CCSS) (Council of Chief State School Officers & National Governors Association Center for Best Practices, 2010).

Mining Purpose	Connection to Standards
How is this reader distinguishing main ideas from supporting details?	**CCSS.ELA-LITERACY.RI.6.2** Determine a central idea of a text and how it is conveyed through particular details. **CCSS.ELA-LITERACY.W.6.8** Gather relevant information from multiple print and digital sources.
How is this reader verifying that the information is credible?	**CCSS.ELA-LITERACY.RI.6.8** Trace and evaluate the argument and specific claims in a text, distinguishing claims that are supported by reasons and evidence from claims that are not.
How is this reader synthesizing information across more than one text or experience?	**CCSS.ELA-LITERACY.RI.6.9** Compare and contrast one author's presentation of events with that of another. **CCSS.ELA-LITERACY.RI.6.7** Integrate information presented in different media or formats (e.g., visually, quantitatively) as well as in words to develop a coherent understanding of a topic or issue.

Mining Purposes: Connection to Standards

STEP 2: OBSERVE THE READER

The second step as a miner is to observe the reader in action. It can be so tempting to skip observation and go straight to asking questions, but observations tell me so much about a reader's level of engagement and her process. Observation is also crucial because it helps refine my purpose by giving me initial data to get curious about, which in turns helps me sharpen the questions I will ask. For example, I recently spent time in a seventh-grade classroom and decided to observe a boy named Dante with the purpose of learning about how he was interpreting his book. He was reading *The Maze Runner* by James Dashner and was flipping through the pages so quickly. He seemed to spend about twenty

seconds per page before turning to the next one. These observations helped guide my curiosity and the questions I wanted to ask him about his reading process (Step 3).

I may observe readers to uncover information about their reading pace, if they are reacting to the text, if and how they write about their reading, or if there are observable behaviors such as moving their lips (subvocalizing) or tracking with their finger. I don't use the observations to form judgments but instead use them to form questions I may ask the reader. My purpose guides what I choose to look for, but I don't let my purpose narrow my vision so much that I ignore other observations that may be important. The following chart shows some general areas of observations with examples of what I may look for.

Area of Observation	What I May Look For
Visible behaviors	• Pointing to words • Tracking with a finger or object • Subvocalizing • Stopping frequently to look away from the text • Stopping to close eyes • Stopping to talk to someone else • Looking at charts or visuals in the classroom • How long it takes them to read a page
Reacting to the text	• Making faces that show emotion • Talking back to a character or author • Jotting reactions on sticky notes in the book
Writing about reading	• Are they stopping to write? • What are they writing? • How are they writing? • How long does it take them to write?

Observing Readers

STEP 3: ASK PROCESS-ORIENTED QUESTIONS

The third step as a miner is to ask the reader questions and have a discussion about what the reader is doing as well as how and why. For many students, it can be difficult to discuss their reading process. Instead, they may talk about the details of the book—they may be stuck in retelling mode. Sometimes this happens as a result of the questions we ask them. While it can be helpful to know if our students can retell their books, I often want to find out much more about them as readers. I want to know what they do as readers, not what the characters in their books do.

- What are you working on as a reader today?
- Can you show me what you are working on?
- If I did not come over and interrupt your reading, what would you be doing right now?
- What is going well for you as a reader?
- Can you describe your reading process right now?

Questions That Frame Reading as a Process

The questions I ask frame the way readers think about their reading process. If I start by asking, "Would you tell me about your book?" I am setting students up to retell. So I should not be surprised when the answer I get is a long and detailed page-by-page summary of the book. If, on the other hand, I begin by asking, "What are you working on as a reader today?" I am setting the student up to think about and share his process. In this case, I may hear the student say something about his purpose for reading, his intentions, and his strategies. Using the list at left as a guide, consider the types of questions you ask if you want to get beyond retelling and summary.

I suggest we ask questions that help us get a glimpse into our students' reading minds. Process-oriented questions also demonstrate to students that naming our reading process is helpful in our path toward becoming more independent and deep-thinking readers.

The three most active parts of being a miner are setting a purpose, observing, and asking process-oriented questions. The table on the next page shows examples of mining purposes from different units of study and the way they guide our questions and observations as miners. Notice how each step of being a miner connects.

STEP 4: LISTEN

The fourth step I take as a miner is to listen. This might sound obvious, but I know there have been many times when I asked someone a question and barely

Step 1: Set a Purpose	Step 2: Observe	Step 3: Ask Process-Oriented Questions
How is this reader distinguishing main ideas from supporting details?	Look at notes and notice if they are organized in ways that show main ideas and details—for example, main ideas in a box and details bulleted out underneath them.	What are some of the main ideas in this article? Can you show how you figured it out?
How is this reader using knowledge of genre to read a text?	Look for the reader to locate specific parts of the text when describing how genre influenced the reading.	What genre is this text? Can you show how the genre's characteristics influence how you read it?
How is this reader comparing characters across texts?	Look for notes on characters, possibly charts or visuals, and also how the reader looks back and references different parts of the books.	How is this character similar to and different from the character in the other book you recently read? Can you show how you compare them?

Three Parts of Being a Miner

listened to her response. Listening is an art in and of itself and an essential step in uncovering readers' processes. If I think back to the two admiring girls at the beach, their entire process shifted when they stopped digging deeply and aggressively and took a moment to sit back and really look and listen. They moved from close-up intensity to wide-angle looking and listening. At first, they were so focused on finding a crab they were missing the clues that were making it almost visible. I often feel this way when talking to readers. If I ask narrow questions and listen only for whether they tell me what I want to hear, I may be missing the clues about what the readers are actually doing and how it is going for them.

With each question I ask during conferring, I work hard to listen to the fullest of my ability. When I listen, I try to keep three essential areas in mind:

1. I remember to bring an admiring lens to what I listen for. That means I listen for what the reader is doing or almost doing, not for what he is not doing or cannot seem to do. I listen for what is there. I listen to name the steps and actions the reader took. If I expect or want to see something in his process that is not there, I can note that, but I don't want to be so distracted by what I am not seeing that I miss the steps the reader is taking.

2. I also use listening as a tool for uncovering the type of mindset a student is working within. I try to understand whether a growth or fixed mindset is shaping her reading process today. As I listen, micro questions tick through my mind: Did the way I framed the question just now inadvertently make this child feel cornered or deficient? Is the child's mindset fixed, and how might I now rephrase the question to see if it can unearth a more confident growth mindset response from this student about this aspect of his process? Or is this child's "can-do" reflection about her process in line with what I've observed? How can I guide her to use strategies that help her actual reading ability catch up to the kinds of texts and levels of understanding she so confidently strives to master?

3. When I listen to a student's response to my question, I keep reading *process* at the forefront and try not to go into judgment mode. By keeping my focus on the reader's process, I listen for what she is doing, why she is doing it, and how she is doing it. This does not mean I decide if what she is doing is good or bad, but instead means I try to listen to get clues about her invisible process of reading and making meaning of the text. I can't decide how to support this reader until after I have uncovered her reading process (see the chart on the next page).

STEP 5: COLLECT

The final step as a miner is to collect all that I uncovered about this reader and document it in some way. I personally tend to document what I uncovered by taking handwritten notes, but I know many teachers who like to use a data-collecting app. What matters most is what I choose to collect more than how I organize it or write it down, as those are personal decisions based on how each teacher likes to stay organized. I am a jotter, note taker, and list maker.

Since uncovering a reader's process involves being a miner, I tend not to collect the nuggets I find in checkboxes or rubrics. Those tools feel too confining,

Element of Listening	Guiding Question	What I Listen For
Asset Lens	What is this reader already doing or approximating?	• The reader's explanation about what he reads and how he reads • What this reader can already do independently • The choices this reader makes on his own
Mindset	What type of mindset is shaping this reader's experience right now?	• If and how this reader labels himself • How this reader talks about struggle and challenges • How this reader talks about goals and growth
Process	What, why, and how is this student reading? What is this reader's process right now?	• The steps this reader takes in his reading process • The reader's purpose for reading and how it impacts the way he reads • The strategies the reader chooses to use and when he chooses them

narrow, and judgment-based at this point in the mining process. If I was working with a student for the purpose of grading her, I might use a rubric or checklist, but since that is not my purpose as a miner, I would not use them now. My notes tend to include lists of questions and theories I created about the reader and jotted-down notes that document my observations and important parts of the reader's process. I also tend to underline, bold, or star particularly important pieces of information I have collected and want to be able to easily refer back to. I use my notes over time to really uncover patterns in how a student reads. By

These are notes about one student's reading mindset and process. I took these notes after being a miner trying to uncover what he already knew how to do when reading. I also wrote down questions I had about his process. These notes do not include my judgments or opinions about the process but instead list the observable behaviors.

Student: **Jayson**

Focus	What Was Uncovered
mindset 9/30	- asked for help at challenging words *(Does he need strategies? Fear of challenge?)* - gave up after 1st attempt - seemed to avoid hard parts
process 10/5	- went back + forth between pictures + words a lot - laughed at funny parts - reacts! - flipped back to pages to connect what made his reactions happen

Gravity Goldberg

collecting notes and rereading them frequently, I can begin to uncover more than simply treating each conversation with a student as brand-new. Trends emerge, and more and more is made visible.

Uncovering One Student's Reading Process

A group of teachers and I sat on the carpet in a fourth-grade classroom as I was about to begin a reading conference. Our intention was to learn ways to uncover students' reading processes one reader at a time. It was about one month into the school year, and the students in this class were toward the end of a unit of study focused on getting to know themselves and setting goals as readers. One teacher turned to me and said, "How do we even start?" I thought for a moment and replied, "We need to get clear on our purpose: What do we want to uncover? Then we watch, and we ask about what we see." In some ways, it is really that simple. I chose a young girl, Susan, to start with. I explained to the teachers, "Since this is my first time working with these readers, my purpose is rather broad. I want to understand how each reader sets goals and approaches the goals." I brought my gaze over to Susan's reading nook and got curious. I began to notice and name what I saw. This is not unlike how I was prepared to be a researcher.

MINER

Student: **Celena**   Unit of Study: **Informational Reading + Research**

Observations	Questions and Curiosities
11/20 • copies facts from the articles onto sticky notes	• Does she understand what she is writing?
11/23 • explains what she is learning to her partner – can tell, show, and describe new info to her	• can this partner talk help her note-taking style?
12/1 - sorts and names a category that info fits in - box and bullets works for her organizing ☐ - all of her talk focuses on the facts she learned	• Does she see the "so what" + bigger purpose of her research?

Patterns: Her process right now seems like:

Read → Take Notes → Talk → Read → Organize Notes

★ How could her thinking + ideas be incorporated in a meaningful way?

Gravity Goldberg

These notes are focused on one student over time. I observed with an admiring lens and wrote down what she already seemed to do, and then I jotted down my questions to pursue later. Because there are many students in a class, the notes allow me to remember what I uncovered and to pick up where I left off in the next conference. I reread my notes to find patterns I can share with the reader.

Several years earlier, while a doctoral student at Teachers College, Columbia University, I took my first qualitative research methods course. My professor explained that one of the first steps to becoming a skilled researcher, the kind who uncovered interesting findings, was to be able to observe closely. She asked us to leave the classroom and find a place to observe. I went over to the steps outside of the main entrance. I wrote down everything I saw. When I returned,

Observations

* reading 1 page in less than 1 minute

* no sticky notes or other notes

* sitting on knees on the chair and moving from side to side a lot

Observation Notes

she explained that we needed to learn to separate observation from interpretations. I reread my notes and realized that many of them were actually my own interpretations of what I saw but not what actually happened.

In this current moment with Susan and her fourth-grade peers, I found myself observing closely and jotting notes. My notes looked like the example at left.

I jotted these observations after less than a minute. I pointed out what I noticed to the teachers who were studying with me in that classroom. "I have so many questions after observing Susan." I forced myself not to jump to interpretations or judge the observation that she did not outwardly appear to be doing what I taught the class in that day's minilesson or what the teacher had been teaching over the past few weeks. Instead I got curious.

I approached Susan, sat down next to her, and said, "Is it OK if I interrupt you?" She nodded.

"So, what are you working on today as a reader?" This was a genuine question I had as it was not evident from observing her what she was working on.

"Well," she said, "honestly, I am just trying to finish this book as fast as possible."

"Oh!" I was surprised by this response. I love being surprised by readers. It reminds me again and again how important it is to admire and uncover what they actually do independently. "I am so curious. Why are you trying to finish this book so fast? Do you not like it?" I asked.

"No, I like it," she said.

"Then why are you trying to rush through it?" I was confused.

"Because when we finish books in this class, we take a test and get points. I want the points!" She smiled at me.

The teachers around me openly gasped at this comment. I chuckled. I always appreciate the honesty and apparent lack of filter that many young readers have. If they just tell me what they think I want to hear, it is so much harder to uncover what is really going on.

"How does that impact how you read books when you are wanting to finish fast and take tests to get points?" I asked.

"Well," she paused to consider this. "I am not sure."

"Today in the minilesson I showed you how I keep track of my thoughts as I read and jot them down quickly. That way, I am prepared for conversations with other readers about my thinking." She nodded as I recapped the lesson. "How do you keep track of your thinking when you read?"

"I don't," she said. "I do have thoughts, but I just keep going because I want to read a lot of pages each day."

"Can you show me a place where you had a thought today when you were reading?" I prompted.

"Sure." She turned back a page. "Right here I was thinking about the character. I was thinking she was not telling the truth." She pointed to the bottom right side of the page.

"And how did you come up with that idea?" I was still curious.

She began flipping pages rapidly back to find an earlier part of the book. Her brows furrowed, and she kept flipping back and forth between pages. "I can't find the part. There was a part around here where this character said the opposite of what she was saying in the later part." She could not show me this character's apparent lie because she could not find the part in her book. Susan laughed and explained, "I am annoyed! I can't find that part now, so I think it would help me find important parts if I marked them. I even have sticky notes in my desk; I just don't ever use them."

If we go back and look at the questions I asked Susan, they all were geared toward understanding her process and intentions as a reader. Here are a few of the questions I asked her in this conversation:

- So, what are you working on today as a reader?
- Why are you trying to finish this book so fast?
- How does that impact how you read books?
- How do you keep track of your thinking when you read?
- Can you show me a place where you had a thought today when you were reading?
- How did you come up with that idea?

I spent time trying to uncover this reader's process. I observed, asked process-oriented questions, and looked at some of her notebook entries. My goal was to try to get inside her reading mind and really understand the nuanced moves she made.

Wendy Murray

When I look at this list, I notice right away that the questions are about how she reads the way she does and why she reads the way she does. Questions that include *how* and *why* help us uncover the reader's process and intentions.

I also noticed I did not ask assignment-based questions that were focused on my agenda as the teacher. For example, I did not ask, "Did you use the strategy I taught you today? Why not?" Or, "I need you to show me the evidence for a character trait because that is what we are all focusing on today in reading." These types of questions are more about checking to see if the student did my assignment than they are about uncovering a process. With Susan, for example, I uncovered her process and then in a sense let her discover that there were things she could do to make her reading experience more satisfying.

If I want to know whether or not a reader used a strategy I taught, I will simply give an actual assessment such as ask everyone to take the last three minutes of our read aloud time to write down a character's trait and explain it with evidence. I will tell students this is for me to see how they are doing with this skill. I carefully carve out small amounts of time across the week to assess and let that be a more formal assessment time. The rest of the time when students are reading, it is their time to own their own process.

Making Sure I Am Uncovering and Not Correcting

If I am having teacher-centered oral quizzes instead of reader-centered conversations, it feels and sounds completely different. I make sure not to turn my questions into a cor-recting and fixing session. If I was to

One-Right-Answer Questions

- What is the setting in Chapter 3?
- How old is the character?
- Did she want to leave her home?

Multiple-Choice Questions

- Did she feel lucky, jealous, or frustrated?
- Was this happening in the past, present, or future?
- Do you think he will listen to his friends, make up his own mind, or do part of what his friend said?

Fill-in-My-Blank Questions

- So she was upset with him because _____
- The mom is at the _____

Correcting and Fixing Questions

approach students thinking they needed to be corrected and fixed, I would ask questions with right answers; I would offer multiple choices; and I would ask them to fill in *my* blanks. The list above shows examples of correcting and fixing questions. This is not what I suggest if your intention is to become a miner. Yet I know it can be very difficult to break our patterns if we are in the habit of asking these sorts of questions.

When having a conversation with Susan, I did not ask any of these types of questions because my intention was not to correct her. Notice the difference between a question like "Can you show me a place where you made a claim about the character today when you were reading?" and one like "Did the main character lie in Chapter 3?" The second "right answer" question would give me such limited information. I would find out if she understood this one part of her book. If she did, I would likely feel good that she was understanding this part. I would have no idea how she made meaning in her book, and therefore, I would not be able to reinforce her process. If she answered the question incorrectly, all I would know was that she did not understand this part of the book. Again, I would not know where her misunderstanding came in and how her reading process was not working for her. I would have no idea what to teach her.

Besides the fact that one-right-answer, multiple-choice, and fill-in-my-blank questions give us such limited insight into a reader's process, they also set a tone that often limits learning. Brain imaging has shown us what happens when humans feel threatened (The Hawn Foundation, 2011). An oral quiz with the teacher who is looking to correct you is threatening to many students. When the brain perceives a threat, the amygdala gets activated. This is part of our primal brain, the part that goes into flight, fight, or freeze to get away from the perceived threat. If a student's amygdala is in flight, fight, or freeze mode, she is likely not going to show all she can do, and she is also physically unable to learn and perform. When the amygdala is activated, the rest of the brain—notably the hippocampus (memory center) and the prefrontal cortex (problem-solving and higher-level-thinking area)—is virtually shut off (The Hawn Foundation, 2011). This is not a recipe for thoughtful reading work and an opportunity for learning. It is not just a nice idea to have students feel safe and comfortable in a conversation with us; it is about optimal conditions for brain functioning and reading.

If Susan was feeling unsafe, she may have shut down in our conversation. Shutting down looks different with each person. Some readers shut down by avoiding the experience. *I have to go to the bathroom. I can't find my book. So-and-so is bothering me.* Others shut down by freezing. This may look like shrugging shoulders, blank stares, or "I don't knows." Still others get angry and outright refuse. *I am not going to do that. I can't. I won't.* Conversations that feel safe from reader to reader create an environment where our full brains can be used. I think we all need that. When we become the miner from a place of admiring readers, it can help readers feel safe and allow them to participate in helping us uncover their reading processes.

If we look at my interactions with Susan, we can see the five steps of being a miner. First, I set a purpose for what I was trying to uncover: her goals for herself as a reader. Second, I observed Susan, noted what she was doing, and got curious. Third, I asked Susan process-oriented questions such as "What are you working on today as a reader?" Fourth, I listened to what Susan could articulate about her process. I heard her explain how and why she reads so fast. Finally, I collected what I uncovered and jotted down notes about Susan's reading process. All five of these steps took about two and a half minutes during part of a reading conference. While I did give Susan feedback and do some teaching, I will save that for the next chapters when we look at our other roles as teachers. This part highlighted what I did as a miner.

Uncovering a Class's Reading Processes

Sometimes we want to gather information about the entire class's reading processes and cannot wait to get that information during one-on-one conferences. If this is the case, we may use a shared reading experience to be a miner of the entire class. Let's step into a sixth-grade class that is at the very beginning of a unit of study that focuses on interpreting lessons from characters' experiences and providing textual evidence to support those interpretations. Notice how the same five-step process can help us be miners in group settings and not just one-on-one.

Kevin called the students over to the meeting area and asked them to bring a clipboard, pencil, and piece of paper. First, he set a clear purpose for being a miner with the class and explained it to them. "Today I am going to read you a folktale called *The Elephant's Nose,* and you are going to do some thinking, writing, and discussing so I can start to uncover how you go about interpreting lessons from characters' experiences. I am not going to think aloud and support your thinking in today's reading because I want to use this as a chance to uncover what you do as readers and how you do it. Please try your best to show how you think about this story." Kevin was clear with the class and with himself that he was trying to uncover how the students went about interpreting lessons from characters' experiences. While he might end up uncovering many other things about the readers in this class, this was his main focus.

Next, Kevin asked the students to fold their papers into four boxes and number them 1, 2, 3, and 4. As he read, he would stop and ask them to do some thinking and writing in each box as a way for him to get inside their reading minds a bit more. Kevin projected the story on the board and began reading the folktale. He stopped after a short bit and asked, "What are you thinking about the character, Elephant, right now? Please jot what you are thinking in box number 1." Each student began writing. Kevin used this writing time as an opportunity to observe his students. He had a note-taking sheet and clipboard, and on one side it showed a box with each student's name and room for notes. The back side was blank for class notes and observations. Kevin noted who was looking back at the projected story on the board, who closed their eyes as they read, and who wrote only a few words and looked timidly around the room. Whatever he noticed during the observation was not corrected or judged, but simply documented.

After two minutes, Kevin continued reading the next portion of the folktale. He stopped again, and this time he asked, "What are your thoughts about the character, Elephant, now? Please take a minute to jot them in box number 2." Again, Kevin observed his class and took more notes. He noticed who was using the word *because* and providing evidence for their thinking. Since this is a short folktale, Kevin finished the story and asked, "Now that we have finished the story, what lessons did you learn from the character Elephant's experiences? Please write about this in box number 3."

As students began finishing their writing, Kevin asked the students to do some more thinking, this time to uncover their process even more. "Now think about *how* you came up with those thoughts about the character, Elephant, and how you interpreted lessons. Describe your process in box number 4."

Each question that Kevin asked was carefully planned out and meant to uncover the readers' process. He was trying to figure out what they thought and how they came up with it. The first three questions were aimed at mining for what students thought, and the final question was aimed at how they formed their thoughts—about naming their processes.

When students were done with this final jot, Kevin asked the students to turn to their partners and explain the lessons the character learned and how they interpreted them. Kevin walked around listening to as many readers discuss their thinking as he could. He now had written work to look at and help him uncover what each reader did when trying to interpret lessons from characters' experiences. As he read each reader's work, he made brief notes about what the reader seemed to do. For example, one note about a student read, "Listed character traits and used character dialogue as evidence. Interpreted lesson by making a claim about the trait's impact on the character." This note does not judge what the reader did but names the process. Kevin spent one period looking at the students' responses and collecting notes to uncover more about their process. He will use this information to plan what and how he teaches this unit of study to this group of readers.

If we look at Kevin's experiences with his students, we can see each of the five steps he took to be a miner:

1. First, he set a clear purpose for what he was trying to uncover, and he even explained it to the class.

2. Second, he observed his students as they thought and jotted each time.

3. Third, he asked process-oriented questions throughout the shared reading experience.

4. Fourth, he listened when they discussed their interpretations and process.

5. Fifth, he collected notes about what he was uncovering both during and after the experience. While whole class assessments are never as specific as one-on-one assessments, this did offer Kevin much more insight into how his students interpreted characters' experiences, and he uncovered much about their thinking and process in a relatively short amount of time. This information impacted his decisions about what and how to teach next.

Kevin and I discussed this process of being a miner, and we decided he could add one more question to this mining experience: Describe one challenging part of the reading work you did today and what you learned from the challenge. We added this question because we wanted to get some insight into readers' mindsets. The next chart shows a few sample responses readers gave that are sorted into growth and fixed mindset categories. This information allowed Kevin to uncover readers' mindset around interpreting lessons as well as their reading process.

Growth Mindset Responses	Fixed Mindset Responses
It was hard to write the lesson because I could not think of the way to say it. I learned you have to try to say it a few different ways for it to be clear.	Nothing was too hard for me because I am a good reader.
A challenge was when I had to write down the thought in box 1 because we had not read very much yet and I did not know what to say. I learned to take a chance and write any idea since I could go back and change it later when I had read more.	I understood it all. Don't worry; there was nothing too hard.
	I'm not a great reader, so I struggled a lot with understanding this.
	It was hard for me, so I started to give up.

Uncovering a Reader's Mindset

Choosing When to Be a Miner

Being a miner means taking instructional time to uncover what is already there. As teachers who have pressure to teach a curriculum and meet standards, it can be anxiety producing to take instructional time to mine. In my experience and in recent research (Hattie, 2012), taking the time to get into the minds of our students saves us time in the long run because we can meet students where they are and build on what they already know and already do. That being said, I do tend to choose carefully when to be a miner instead of taking on other roles.

I choose to be a miner when I am starting something new such as a new unit, a new genre, or working with a new group. When students or topics are new, I want to uncover what they already know and do first to help me plan for instruction. I also choose to be a miner when I am conferring with readers. I almost always begin reading conferences as a miner and take the first few minutes to get to know the individual reader in front of me. One-on-one time is a gift, and I want to make sure I get to know every reader's process and how it is evolving

When students are talking about their books, it is an opportunity to uncover their reading preferences. I take advantage of this opportunity by listening to conversations and noticing what they talk about and how they talk, and try to uncover their tastes. This means I don't interrupt and take over the conversation. I sit back and listen. I might learn who tends to love long descriptions with challenging vocabulary and who prefers action-packed stories with a bit of tension.

Gravity Goldberg

across the year. Finally, I tend to be a miner with small groups of students when I am trying to figure out where to go next with them. This might be a group of students who are already quite advanced and skilled in an area, and I want to uncover what I can teach them next. Or this might be a group of readers who are far below grade level, and I want to figure out where to start so they can build confidence with what they already can do and go from there. Anytime I am curious or in need of knowing what is going on inside students' reading minds, I can become a miner.

Admiring Trouble

A repeating section in the next few chapters is called *Admiring Trouble* where I show you how perceived problems that arise in reading classrooms can be turned around and used as learning opportunities for us to admire. I deliberately chose the term *trouble* because to me it seems truer to any practitioner's day-to-day work experiences than the more often used, softer term *challenge*. For example, I wouldn't turn to a colleague in the faculty room and say, "I'm challenged to figure out why my fourth graders are struggling with theme so much." I'd say, "I'm having trouble figuring out . . ." The following examples are trouble spots most of us have encountered time and time again.

THE "TROUBLE"

Each day after the reading minilesson, three students wait at the meeting area and ask, "What are we supposed to do today?" It seems as if these readers simply sit and daydream during the entire minilesson and have no idea what has just been taught. The trouble is that if I take the time to reteach the minilesson again right now to these few students, I am using my conferring and small group time, and I am sending the message that it is OK for them to ignore the minilesson because I will teach it again. But, if I don't reteach the lesson, they end up sitting in class and not doing anything. This is a frustrating pattern many of us experience.

EXAMINING THE "TROUBLE" WITH AN ADMIRING LENS

My first reaction might be "These students do not pay attention." While this may or may not be true, when I react this way, I end up becoming more frustrated and often narrow my vision so much I cannot admire what the readers are doing. Instead of focusing solely on what these students seem to *not* be doing, I can get curious about what they are doing during the minilesson. I can be a miner and use the five steps to uncover what is going on rather than assume they are not paying attention. When I know what students are not doing, it is part of the picture, but I also want to know what they are doing.

WHAT I DID

I set a purpose: What are these readers' processes for learning during and directly after a minilesson? I called these students over to the meeting area two minutes early and let them know the purpose, not to scold or warn them, but to enlist their help in uncovering their processes. I explained, "I noticed that after the minilesson you often are unclear about what I just taught and need help deciding what to do. I want to help you by trying to understand your learning process during the minilesson. Can you try to pay attention to what you do during and right after the minilesson, and we will meet briefly to discuss it?"

During the minilesson, I observed each of the three students. I noticed who looked at me, who stared around the room, and who sat where. During the guided-practice part of the minilesson, I listened to these students so I could hear what they said. When I got to the link portion at the end of the minilesson, I looked directly at each of the three students and gave them all a minute to set their intentions for reading time today. These three students remained at the meeting area while the others went back to start reading.

I asked process-oriented questions, and the four of us had a conversation about what they found out about their process during the minilesson. I asked the following questions:

- What did you notice about what you did during the minilesson?
- What seemed to help you learn?
- What might be getting in the way of you learning?
- Do you have any ideas about what is and is not working for you?

Since I had enlisted these students' help prior to the minilesson, they could answer some of these questions, and they are used to having honest conversations about their process.

WHAT I LEARNED

As I listened to what the readers explained about their process, I realized that they were each doing many things during the minilesson that were previously invisible to me and that it was much more complicated than "they are not paying attention." I learned that these students were paying attention, but not necessarily to what was most helpful to their learning. One reader explained that he did not like the book I was demonstrating from. He seemed to be focused on the content of my book, and he was paying attention. He paid attention to the book, and when he found the book boring, he paid attention to his own opinions and reactions to it. By uncovering this reader's process, I was able to see what he was doing as a reader and discuss how it was going for him.

Together we realized that his opinions about a book matter and that they also can end up distracting him from what I was demonstrating in the minilesson. We acknowledged his strengths at reacting and forming opinions about books, and we admired this part of his reading process. Even though we did not leave that one conversation with a magic bullet, I was no longer frustrated with the students. I was able to admire what they were doing, and we had more information we could uncover during the next few days' lessons. I learned that admiring readers means you work *with* students as a team to uncover what they do and how they do it. We were coresearchers and collaborators, and together we were actively engaged in figuring out what was going on.

Conclusion

The final chart in this chapter shows each step of being a miner along with its characteristics. When taking on a new or unfamiliar role, it can help to look at what that role entails and to compare it with what it is not. You can use this chart to reflect on the steps you take when being a miner in your classroom and which ones you may want to refine.

MINER

Step	What It Is	What It Is Not
Set a purpose	Deciding on a clear focus before beginning to mine	Assessing whatever the day's lesson might have been or having no focus at all
Observe the reader	Taking time to see what the reader is doing and becoming curious about the reader	Looking for something to fix or change
Ask process-oriented questions	Having a discussion that helps uncover *how* a student reads and allows the reader to show you what he does	Quizzing the student on the content of the book or the day's lesson
Listen	Being open to what the reader has to teach you about his own process and mindset	Correcting and fixing any mistakes you hear
Collect	Documenting what I just did and learned about the reader	Forming judgments and fitting readers into a checkbox

Reflection Chart When Being a Miner

Uncovering a reader's process is an act of pure curiosity. If we approach students as miners and take time to look at and listen to them, they can teach us a great deal about what they already know how to do. Admiring readers is about taking time to really see and really hear what every reader can teach us. In our rush to work with as many students as possible and our stress about standards and testing, it can seem unwise to take the time not only to get the gist of a reader's process but to actually admire it. But if we settle for the gist of who they are as readers, we may be missing so much they are already doing that we can build upon. Sometimes the key to uncovering what readers are doing is to step back a little bit, like the girls at the beach, and observe first. It was when the girls took their time and went gently layer by layer into the sand that they uncovered their purpose and began to admire.

In the next chapter, we take on the role of mirror and look at how we evaluate what we mine and then can give feedback to readers. The type of feedback and the way we offer it can help each reader grow. Our feedback creates a relationship to readers that can support a growth mindset where they develop more aware-ness, confidence, and ownership.

Andrew Levine Photography

Andrew Levine Photography

Be a Mirror

Giving Feedback That Reinforces a Growth Mindset

In the previous chapter, we learned to take on the role of a miner, uncovering readers' process with a five-step approach. The steps included setting a purpose, observing, asking process-oriented questions, listening, and collecting the information we found. In this chapter, we will learn about the role of a mirror and specific ways our feedback to readers can support a growth mindset where readers feel ownership for what they are already doing.

Feedback is essential for learning and engagement. Brene Brown (2012), a social worker, writer, and professor, researches shame and vulnerability and how we can create organizational cultures that help people "show up" and engage. She explains just how important feedback is. "Without feedback there can be no transformative change. When we don't talk to the people we're leading about their strengths and their opportunities for growth, they begin to question their contributions and our commitment. Disengagement follows" (Brown, 2012, p. 197). Brown goes on to explain how rare valuable feedback can be. "Today's organizations are so metric-focused in their evaluation of performance that giving, receiving, and soliciting valuable feedback ironically has become rare. It's even a rarity in schools where learning depends on feedback, which is infinitely more effective than grades scribbled on the top of a page or computer-generated, standardized test scores" (Brown, 2012, p. 197).

When others reflect back to us what they see, it gives us another perspective, whether as a reader, a cook, or a photographer. I notice that feedback can either promote a fixed mindset—"You are a great cook"—or be too general to be helpful—"This photograph is lovely." When meeting one of my friends recently for dinner, she looked at me quickly and said, "You look so nice." I noticed that this feedback made me feel good, but then left me a bit flat. I wondered, "What is nice about the way I look? How can I look nice like this again?" My friend was being thoughtful and kind when giving the feedback, and I appreciated it. Since she is a good friend, I felt comfortable following up with her, "What do you mean? Can you be more specific?" She smiled at me, knowing I am a teacher and writer and often have these types of requests. She explained, "Well, you have that burnt orange scarf on, and that color brings out your highlights. Also, when you wear a scarf wrapped and draped in this way, it creates a soft shape that frames your face." Now I had real feedback I could use. In the first comment, I was left wondering how to re-create what seemed to be working for me. When she gave feedback the second time, I knew specifically what I could do, namely wear burnt orange and drape scarves around my neck.

This example is a bit superficial and silly, but it does translate to reading instruction too. When we sit with students and give feedback that sounds like this—"Great job reading today!"—it is the equivalent of saying, "You look nice today." It is too general to be helpful feedback. Also, I must admit, when someone tells me, "You look nice today," I always wonder whether this is unusual and needs to be pointed out. Is it code for "Wow, today you actually look nice"? I wonder if, when we tell readers, "You did a great job reading today," they too feel it comes across as a surprise. Just like the specific feedback about the color and scarf, we can offer readers much more specific feedback that helps mirror for them what they actually are doing and how it seems to be working for them. Imagine instead of the general "good job" compliment we said, "When you paused and thought about why the character was making that decision, it seemed to help you connect the previous events to the conflict." This sort of feedback is specific and something the reader can continue to do when needed.

Feedback Teaches

When we are being a mirror and giving readers specific and growth mindset feedback, we are not just helping readers feel confident but also teaching them. Many readers are not aware of everything they do as they read, nor are they aware of how it may be helping or hindering their process. When we take the time to give feedback based on what we saw when we were the miner, readers have much more awareness of their process and how they can use strategies again when needed. Readers may struggle to transfer a strategy from one situation to the next because they are not aware of how it is impacting what they are doing and they may not have language yet to name it. We can mirror back what we notice and name it for them, along with ideas for when they may choose to use the strategies in future and possibly more complex reading experiences. Peter Johnston (2004) describes the importance of students noticing and naming what they do. He explains, "When children notice things, instruction can begin with a joint focus of attention because the children are already attending" (Johnston, 2004, p. 18). Our feedback brings students' attention to what, how, and why they tend to read.

MIRROR

Feedback that teaches has five qualities, listed at right. It is **specific** and names what the reader did. It is **asset-based** and focuses on what the reader already is doing that is helping. In addition, it is **growth mindset–based** and describes the effort and work the reader put in, not just the end product. It can be transferred from one reading experience to another. Finally, feedback that teaches is helpful when it is **nonjudgmental** and sticks to neutral statements about what the reader did without our "shoulds" or "I need you to's." Feedback supports ownership when we don't make it about ourselves and keep our focus on the reader.

Five Qualities of Feedback:
1. Be specific.
2. Name what is.
3. Focus on the process.
4. Make sure it can transfer.
5. Take yourself out of it.

Preparing to Give Feedback

It can be challenging to give feedback if we don't feel prepared. Preparation involves knowing each reader well, having already been a miner and uncovering what our students do as readers. If we have not yet uncovered what readers do, we can only give overly general feedback such as "good job today." If we want to give feedback, we have to uncover first, because if we don't know the intricacies of the reader's process, it will be difficult to notice and name what's happening.

Another, often forgotten, aspect of being ready to give feedback includes our own lens. If we are not taking on an admiring lens and are feeling frustrated with our students, the feedback will likely not be well received or helpful. Brown (2012) created a checklist to reflect on how ready someone is to give feedback. While this checklist is a general one created for leaders in all types of organizations, several of the qualities apply to admiring readers and becoming a mirror. The readiness qualities that apply here include these:

- I want to acknowledge what you do well instead of picking apart your mistakes.
- I recognize your strengths and how you can use them to address your challenges.
- I can hold you accountable without shaming or blaming you.
- I can model the vulnerability and openness that I expect to see from you. (Brown, 2012, p. 204)

Before you begin to be a mirror and give feedback to the readers you work with, reflect on how prepared you are to begin.

QUALITY 1: BE SPECIFIC

Feedback is valuable when it is specific. Since one of my goals as a reading teacher is for students to take what they learned from one reading experience to another, I have to be specific and name what the reader is doing. Yet, I also can't be so specific that the feedback cannot transfer to another experience and only applies to one text. The visual on the next page shows the feedback continuum from too general to too specific. When feedback is just right, it can be applied to other texts and reading experiences.

Making feedback specific includes naming what the reader did and what resulted. The general feedback "Good job predicting" does not name what the reader actually did or its results. It could be turned into specific feedback if it included both parts, the process and the results. Instead I might say, "When you took the time to read the title and headings, scan the images, and think about the topic [the reader's process], it helped you predict what specifically you would be learning about in the article and helped you prepare to learn more about the topic [the results]."

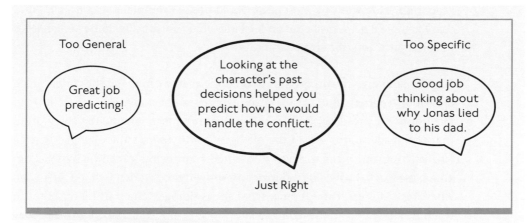

Continuum of Feedback Examples

QUALITY 2: NAME WHAT IS

When admiring is our lens, we focus on what the reader *is doing* and name it for her. If our feedback focuses on what the reader is not doing, it is reinforcing the deficit view and possibly contributing to frustration and confusion. If you were given feedback, would you want it to focus on what the person saw you doing or what he did not see you doing? After all, a mirror can only reflect what is there. Notice the difference between the two examples of feedback below and how you might react to each.

Example A: I noticed you did not change your voice to match the character who was talking. You did not recognize it was dialogue as you read.

Example B: I noticed you read in longer phrases, paused at the end of each sentence briefly, and read at a consistent pace. When you did this, it sounded smooth and helped you make meaning of the story. When it did not sound right, you went back and reread that part until it did make sense, and then you continued on.

Two Examples of Feedback

If you were this reader, which example would you prefer to hear? Which would help you feel seen and your work acknowledged? Which would motivate you to keep it up? I am guessing most of us would prefer Example B. As a reader, I find that Example B helps me better understand what I am already doing, which leads to confidence and ownership.

Readers can't own the things they don't do. A reader can't own the "I don't read dialogue" feedback. But a reader can own "I read at a consistent pace to help me monitor my reading" feedback. This does not mean I ignore the observation that this reader did not read the dialogue. I will address the dialogue when I am teaching and being a model and when I am being a mentor. When I am giving feedback, I am being a mirror and showing the student what *is* there and what she *is* doing. I can even use what she is doing as the starting-off point to teach her how to read the dialogue later. Social work educator Dennis Saleebey describes this as the "strengths perspective" and claims, "Viewing performance from a strengths perspective offers us the opportunity to examine our struggles in light of our capacities, talents, competencies, possibilities, visions, values, and hopes" (quoted in Brown, 2012, p. 199). This strengths perspective is at the core of admiring readers and being a mirror.

QUALITY 3: FOCUS ON THE PROCESS

When giving feedback, it can be tempting to focus on the end result, the product only. Overly focusing on the end result can end up reinforcing a fixed mindset that explains reading as something you are either good at or not. When students hold a fixed mindset about themselves as readers, they end up believing reading proficiency is a static skill regardless of the process or work you put in. Fixed mindset feedback might sound like this: "Great job finding the author's claim and evidence." In this example, the result is the only aspect highlighted and named for the reader. If this reader encounters a challenge the next time he tries to find the author's claim or evidence, he may end up thinking he no longer is good at this, or he may hide his struggle and avoid it. Dweck (2007) explains, "Our research shows that educators cannot hand students confidence on a silver platter by praising their intelligence. Instead, we can help them gain the tools they need to maintain their confidence in learning by keeping them focused on the *process*" (p. 39). Instead of results-only feedback, we can offer process-focused feedback to support a growth mindset.

Process-focused feedback acknowledges and highlights the work the reader did and shows the reader how the work led to learning. It includes the process and the results. Feedback that focuses on the process acknowledges the hard parts and normalizes them. Brown's (2012) research shows the benefits of normalizing discomfort, a finding that led her to explicitly tell people that learning involves work and effort, and can be uncomfortable at times. She offers the following example of what a leader might say. "We believe that growth and learning are uncomfortable so it's going to happen here—you're going to feel that way. We want you to know that it's normal and it's an expectation here. You're not alone and we ask that you stay open and lean into it" (Brown, 2012, p. 198).

Feedback that highlights the work the reader put in might sound like this: "When you saw the repeated phrase in the poem, you noticed it must be important. Then you struggled to figure out why the author was repeating that phrase over and over again. It was not easy for you to see it as a symbol, but you kept rereading it and thinking more about 'What could this mean?' You tried a few different interpretations until you settled on the one that made the most sense given the title and the rest of the poem. Interpreting symbols is a really challenging part of reading and often does take many rereads to come to an idea you can stand by. By putting that work in, you really have a deeper understanding and appreciation of this poem." In this example, the hard work and struggle was not hidden or minimized. It was highlighted because it is the aspect that the reader will need to hold on to—that interpretation of symbols can take a tremendous amount of work but does pay off.

This example shows how growth mindset feedback not only acknowledges but also celebrates the work and the process. Johnston (2012) explains, "Surprisingly small changes in feedback can have quite broad consequences, because the feedback marks whether we are in the fixed-performance world or the dynamic-learning world . . . Process and effort-oriented feedback are the best options" (p. 39). The visual below shows a few more examples of fixed and growth mindset feedback.

Fixed Mindset Compliments
- You are a great reader.
- You are good at _____
- Good readers do _____

Growth Mindset Compliments
★ You stuck with that tricky word and kept working until you figured it out.
★ When you got confused about who was talking, you stopped to envision the characters and that helped you figure it out.

Fixed and Growth Mindset Feedback

QUALITY 4: MAKE SURE IT CAN TRANSFER

If we are taking the time to give feedback to readers, we may want to ensure it can be transferred to other reading experiences. I find that many students, even older ones, don't necessarily see the connections between what we did during reading time and what we do during science time. It can be helpful to help make those connections for students by giving feedback in a way that shows the process is transferrable. This means I tend to include the "when" in feedback and not just the what and how.

Let's look at feedback given to a small group of readers broken down into parts. We already looked at feedback that included the qualities of being specific, naming what is, and focusing on the process. The first two rows of the following chart show these qualities. The third row adds the transfer quality and includes an example of telling readers *when* they might choose to use this process in future reading experiences.

Feedback Quality	What to Consider	What Was Said
Be specific and name what is	*What* did the reader do?	When you finished reading two articles on the same topic, you stopped to compare how they were similar and different.
Focus on the process	*How* did the reader do this?	You reread your notes on the first article and the second article, and you put a check mark next to the notes that were the same in both.
	What were the results?	This helped you make some inferences about what was common knowledge and important.
Make sure it can transfer	*When* might the reader do this again?	Whenever you are reading more than one text or watching more than one video, you can use this process whether it be in science, social studies, or any reading experience where you want to compare information.

Small Group Feedback

By including the "when" in our feedback, we are not leaving to chance that readers will know they can use this process again and when it might be helpful. Many students I have worked with over the years use a strategy during reading time, and then when they are reading for social studies or for mathematics, they don't even consider using the strategy. When I ask students about this, they often tell me, "Oh? I didn't realize I could use it here too." When we include the when, we are setting students up to know that a strategy does transfer and giving them insight into the context in which they might want to choose to use it again.

QUALITY 5: TAKE YOURSELF OUT OF IT

MIRROR

When giving feedback, consider how often you insert yourself into what you say. For years, my feedback started like this: "I like how you . . ." or "I need you to . . ." When I reflected on my choice of language, I realized that I was creating a people-pleasing situation where I made it about me. I don't actually want readers to do things because I like it. I want readers to choose to do things because it helps them. When we insert our judgments into the feedback, we end up inadvertently making reading about us, and the ownership is no longer with the student.

Notice the subtle differences between feedback when it includes the teacher's judgments and feedback when it does not. Feedback that starts off with the teacher judgment sounds like this: "*I like how you* previewed the page before you started reading." Or the same feedback could be given and not include the teacher's judgment, instead including a neutral description of what was done: "You previewed the page before you started reading, and this helped you predict the categories of information you would be learning about." The *I like how you* puts the immediate emphasis on the teacher and not the reader.

When giving feedback, we can also consider where we position ourselves physically in relation to the students. If I am standing up and looking down at the students, I am creating a clear physical representation of our relationship. I am in power and control here. If, on the other hand, I sit at the same level as the students, I am positioning myself as a fellow reader with some feedback to offer. Brown (2012) suggests that all feedback be given with people sitting on the same side of the table. By sitting side by side without a desk or anything bulky in between you and the reader, you are showing you are on the same team and want the same things.

Gail spends time with this reader as a mirror. She looks back at her notes and then offers growth mindset feedback. She sits side by side with the student as a fellow reader.

Gravity Goldberg

Carl Anderson (2005), author and writing consultant, explains, "I no longer use the words *good* and *bad* to describe students and their writing. To me, students are simply somewhere on the path toward becoming lifelong writers. My job is not to judge them but to figure out where they are on the path and then nudge them forward on their journey" (p. 143). Our feedback to readers can serve as that nudge. If we want to give feedback that is valuable and supports a growth mindset, we can practice each of the five qualities. We can be specific, name what is, focus on the process, make sure it can transfer, and take ourselves out of it. Of course, each of these qualities takes practice and time to develop, and I continue to work on them myself.

Being a Mirror to a Small Group

Janine's fourth-grade class had been learning to participate in book clubs for the past week. She spent that time teaching whole class minilessons about how to prepare and participate in a book club as well as being a miner during the independent reading and book club conversation time. She was ready to sit with one of the groups and give some feedback. Since participating in a book club was relatively new to the readers, she wanted to make sure she was mirroring with an admiring lens. This would allow her students to feel ownership for how it was going so far. Janine waited for the club conversation time and sat down in the circle with the readers. She looked at the notes she collected as a miner and asked, "Would you mind if I took the first two minutes of your club time to give you some feedback?" The readers nodded OK.

Having worked with Janine for a few years, I already knew she was a thoughtful teacher and wanted to give feedback that inspired her students. We spent recent coaching sessions observing each other give feedback and reflecting on what seemed to be most valuable. At first, most of our feedback to students was general or about how we "liked how you . . . ," and we consciously decided to offer feedback in different ways. On this particular day, Janine was ready to give feedback to support a growth mindset.

Janine looked at her students and began, "So I have been observing your book club during your conversation time, and I was able to confer with each of you this week during independent reading time. I noticed a pattern. All of you came prepared to the discussion and had notes jotted down, passages marked, and ideas listed that you wanted to talk about. When it came time to have the discussion, you went in a circle, and each person shared all of her ideas and read them like a list. The other members listened and then took their turn sharing. You included everyone, and when you got all the way around the circle, you discussed which ideas seemed similar across the group." The book club members nodded.

Old habits can be hard to break because I found myself as the observer in this room wanting to jump in and point out what they were not doing. But Janine maintained her admiring lens and remembered that being a mirror means reflecting back what readers are doing. So far Janine had described the *what* (coming prepared and including everyone) and *how* (going in a circle and reading their list of ideas), and she was about to add on with the results and the *when*.

"So it seems like when you all share your list of ideas around the circle, every reader gets to be heard, and you have a sense of what everyone was thinking during this section of the book. It allows you to listen to multiple ideas and consider similarities across them," Janine noted, to sum up what they were doing.

"From now on when you are working in a group, even if it is not a book club, you can do this—come prepared with ideas to share and let everyone have space and time to share so you can hear all the ideas," she said to help them transfer. Janine offered this feedback because she understood the importance of gaining multiple perspectives when comprehending a text and she wanted to reinforce that with her students.

By being a mirror, Janine gave her students feedback that included what they were doing, how they were doing it, and when they might want to do it again. Over the next few days, Janine noticed similar trends in her class's book clubs, and she taught minilessons to address next steps for the clubs such as taking turns, sharing ideas in a more authentic way, not feeling they always had to go in a circle when talking, and how to respectfully challenge one another's ideas to seek new interpretations.

These three readers are members of a book club. The students meet regularly to discuss their interpretations and ideas about books. They noticed they needed to do some further research to more deeply understand an issue in their book, so they worked together to conduct a search and find the answers to their questions.

Gravity Goldberg

Being a Mirror to the Whole Class

Janine realized she needed to teach her class how to build on each other's ideas, how to add textual evidence to their discussions, and how to respectfully challenge claims that were not supported in the text. These would be the next days' minilessons. She began today's minilesson with feedback to the entire class as a way to connect what she was about to teach them to what she had noticed as a miner. Whole class feedback has the same qualities as one-on-one or small group feedback.

"Now that we have been meeting in book clubs for a little while, I wanted to share what I have been noticing across the clubs. While each club is a bit different, one common set of behaviors is repeating across them. The clubs are all sharing claims and are willing to share opposing points of view when they arise." She stated *what* the readers were doing.

"It goes something like this." Janine made sure to use her body and face to sort of reenact what she was noticing about *how* they were doing this. "First, a member of the club sits with his book closed and his notes in front of him. The books remain closed. Someone else makes a claim that is different from the first person's claim and reads her notes. The books remain closed. Then a third person in the club adds her point of view about the difference of opinion. Each person then begins talking at the same time and explains why his or her claim is the right one." Janine paused and smiled. She was not sharing this as a reprimand or with any sort of judgment; she was simply explaining what she saw. A few students nodded in agreement or pointed to each other in their clubs as she paused.

She began this class feedback with the *what* and the *how*, and she was about to add the *when*. "When you have the opportunity to read a common text and discuss it with others, it allows you to discuss different claims. It opens you up to new ways of thinking by hearing opposing points of view. If you are in a situation where you have a different idea or can make a different claim from what you have heard, you can share it with the group. This might be during book club time, during whole class conversations about the read aloud, in a social studies debate, or when preparing to write an essay." While there is more these students can learn about how to debate, how to use the text to provide evidence, and how to listen to each other, these are all possible teaching points. At this moment, Janine was giving feedback, not teaching something new.

MIRROR

By starting her minilesson with whole class feedback, she piqued the students' interest and built context so they would see how the day's teaching point connected to their club. Ownership can be supported by giving feedback that connects to teaching. In addition, offering feedback about what the readers are doing is acknowledging all the work they are already doing. Janine acknowledges and mirrors back what her students are learning to do, and this creates a safe space to do even more.

Admiring Trouble

THE "TROUBLE"

I sat with Lisa and found myself completely overwhelmed with what to focus on. I could not think of anything positive to say. When I work with some students who are well below grade level, like Lisa, I find myself with long lists of what they need to learn and a short or almost nonexistent list of what they are already doing well. Lisa is a student who needs a mirror and to have more awareness of what she is doing that is working for her as a reader. Lisa needs to build confidence, transfer strategies, and take on a growth mindset. Yet, when I sit with her in a conference, I feel urgency to tell her what she needs to learn, and I am tempted to offer my long list of strategies and begin teaching them all. If I were to do this, I might end up saying, "Today I need to teach you how to do this . . . and you also need to learn to do this . . . and then let's work on this . . ." If I were to actually focus on all that Lisa needed at once, we would likely both throw our hands in the air and give up. So what can we do for our students who have long lists of needs and are well below grade level?

EXAMINING THE "TROUBLE" WITH AN ADMIRING LENS

My first reaction might be "Lisa needs me to teach her so much I don't have time to find out what she is already doing well. She needs lots of instruction to catch up." Or, if I am particularly overwhelmed, I might even believe "this student isn't doing anything well I can offer feedback about." With an admiring lens, neither of these statements is actually true, but both are more a sign of me being anxious and fearful that I cannot meet her needs. Instead of jumping right into teaching, Lisa likely needs specific and growth mindset feedback. I can take a deep breath and ask myself, "What is this student already doing? How is this student tending to read? What can this student build upon that she currently does?" Every reader is doing something, and I just need to take a moment to uncover it.

WHAT I DID

One practice that has helped me look for and find strengths in readers like Lisa who have many needs is to take notes in a way that reminds me to look for what the reader is already doing well. I have a few different note-taking systems that help me when I am a miner, and they all set me up to be the mirror when giving feedback.

The first example, shown in the chart below, is focused on studying the reader and really understanding and mining what she is doing. I may not give growth mindset feedback for every observation on this list, but it does help me uncover and then give feedback.

After taking these notes, I was prepared to be a mirror. I chose something off my list of observations to mirror and tried to include all five qualities of growth mindset feedback. My feedback was "Lisa, you stopped to think about the character's feelings. You thought the character Annie was feeling annoyed. What helped you to infer the character's feelings was to look at who she was interacting with and how she was interacting with him. You noticed that Jack was stalling and Annie wanted to make a decision. You know that paying attention to what the

Observations: What the Reader *Is* Doing	Notes: What I Am Thinking
Lisa 10/3 • reading in 3- to 4-word phrases • pausing at end punctuation • describing literal information about the character	• could benefit from understanding how to read dialogue to help with comprehension of who is talking to whom
10/9 • inferring character's feelings • some evidence given—mostly personal connections	• could build off of this—using character actions, thinking, etc., to infer character motivation

Observing the Reader as a Miner

character wants is a way to figure out how she is feeling because you can look to see if she is getting it. Then you look to see how she is reacting. By inferring the character's feelings, you are getting a glimpse into what is really going on with the characters, and it helps you understand why they make the decisions they do. From now on when you are reading books with characters, you can continue to think about who the character is interacting with and how, paying special attention to what the character wants and how she is reacting to getting it or not. It will continue to help you understand characters' decisions and actions." After I gave this feedback, Lisa sat up taller and beamed.

Language I Avoid Because It Feels Fixed	Language I Choose Because It Mirrors
Labeling language: *"Good readers . . ."* *"Strong readers . . ."*	**I describe.** *"I noticed . . ."* *"I observed . . ."* *"First you . . . then you . . ."*
Absolute language: *"Always . . ."* *"Never . . ."*	**I confirm what I already know.** *"You love reading fantasies . . ."* *"This reminds me of when . . ."*
Rewarding or reprimanding language: *"You didn't do . . . so you aren't going to get to do . . ."* *"Look at how well this group did . . ."* *"If you get through . . . you will get to . . ."*	**I acknowledge ambiguity.** *"Perhaps . . ."* *"Maybe . . ."* *"Could it be . . . ?"*
Accusatory language: *"You didn't try."* *"You're lazy when it comes to . . ."* *"If you cared about your work, you would . . ."*	**I ask questions about what I observe.** *"How's it going?"* *"What might you need some support with?"* *"What is getting in the way of . . . ?"* *"What do you need?"*

Choosing Feedback Language

WHAT I LEARNED

Approaching all readers, even those who are well below grade level, with an admiring lens means I consciously choose what I am looking for and studying about the reader. When I do this, it helps me to take notes on what *is* already a part of this reader's process. Taking the time to give growth mindset feedback, like the examples in the right-hand column of the chart on the previous page, is a form of teaching and not a luxury to be skipped over to get to real teaching. Readers who have many needs are often the very ones who need feedback that focuses on mirroring what they already do so they can develop the confidence to continue to work toward their goals.

Conclusion

When being a mirror, we can give feedback that serves as a form of teaching and supports a growth mindset. There are five qualities of feedback that contribute to effective feedback, listed below. When giving feedback, remember we can be a mirror and try to include each quality in what we say to readers.

In the next chapter, we will take on the role of the model and examine how we can show students our reading process as a form of explicit instruction. Part of being an admirer of readers is also teaching them additional strategies that they may not currently be using. In Chapter Seven, I will explain each step of being a model and how we can be effective at teaching readers while maintaining their ownership of their own reading lives.

Qualities of Feedback
- Be specific.
- Name what is.
- Focus on the process.
- Make sure it can transfer.
- Take ourselves out of it.

CHAPTER SEVEN

Be a Model
Showing Readers What We Do

YouTube. TED Talks. Popular shows on cooking, remodeling, dancing—you name it. What these examples have in common is that they teach by modeling—a high degree of the "show, don't tell" maxim at work. But there's more to unpack here that we can use to inform our reading instruction. What these offerings and thousands of others like them remind me about teaching and learning is this:

- Humans are highly social beings, and we like to learn in the midst of others, seeing them, hearing their voice and intonation, watching their expressions and movements. We engage in a social contract of sorts as we take in information.
- We learn most efficiently when information or a process is presented with a combination of explaining, demonstration, and naming.
- We can more readily take on the hard work of learning something new when we see that the expert is also engaging in it. Seeing it in action reminds us that it's work worth doing, that it can be mastered, and that yes, even the expert has to "roll up her sleeves" and do it.

MINER

MIRROR

MODEL

MENTOR

Andrew Levine Photography

- As learners, we don't just want fragmented information; we want to be inspired, and we're inspired by seeing combined with the "how to" information.
- We are wired for narrative, and the explaining and naming that occurs is storytelling.

Now let's turn to the more nuts-and-bolts practical reasons we like to learn from *shows*. Well, because they *show*, they often reveal in an instant what fifty words can sometimes fail to convey. For example, take the chef Giada De Laurentiis. I remember the first time I saw her put "a pinch" of salt in a bowl. I was shocked. My idea of a pinch was about a tenth of what I had just witnessed—and I then understood why my cooking often tasted bland. When I watched her beat eggs vigorously, I had a much more specific sense of what *vigorously* meant and realized why there were lumps in my cake batter. Julienne, blanche, reduce a stock; how high the flame is; what caramelized looks like; how to quickly work on another part of the recipe while something cooks . . . I could read, reread, and even look at photos in a cookbook and never fully "get it."

Now think about your students, and the times when you have told them to do something and, well, they couldn't do it. Like "Add a pinch of salt" or "Cook until done," in the past I've told my students, "Read carefully and find the key details," or "As you read this chapter opener, visualize the setting," or "Pay attention to what the characters say." In essence, I've given them recipes that tell them what to do, rather than show them how to do it. And what I was asking students to do was successfully make a highly complex recipe: reading a text. As reading teachers, we can learn so much about how to be clear and explicit models by noticing what cooking show demonstrations look like. When teachers are acting as models, they tend to do three main actions in order to teach readers strategies. These actions include explaining, demonstrating, and naming.

Brian Cambourne (1995), the language and literacy researcher, found seven conditions of learning that must be present for optimal literacy learning to take place. One of these conditions is demonstration, which is explained as "learners need to receive many demonstrations of how texts are constructed and used" (Cambourne, 1995, p. 187). As we read in the previous chapters, readers benefit when their teachers are miners uncovering what they do. Readers also benefit from growth mindset feedback, where their teachers are mirrors. Once we have mined and mirrored, we can begin to add to what readers already know how to do by showing them additional ways of reading. We can take on the role of being a model reader.

Being a Model

Being a model is much more than telling students what I would do or what I did do, or doing a single, brief demonstration. Being a model means I explain a strategy I use, I demonstrate it by using the strategy in front of the students, and then I name what I did and when I choose to use it. It can be easy to confuse modeling with other types of teaching, so I tend to imagine I am in my own television show, but thank goodness I am not teaching cooking—I am teaching reading. I imagine I am starring in *Reading With Gravity* and my job is to explain, demonstrate, and name what I am doing. This is just like when Giada explains, demonstrates, and names what she is doing when she makes breaded chicken cutlets.

ACTION 1: SET THE CONTEXT BY EXPLAINING

When modeling, I begin by explaining what the strategy is and why I would use it. The *why* is important, because when students aren't sure of the purpose, they aren't as inclined to invest in the experience. Setting the context also focuses students; they know what to pay special attention to as they observe my process. When I neglect to explain and just jump into modeling, students sometimes focus on things that are not really important. For example, I once modeled how I figured out the meaning of a specific vocabulary word in an informational picture book. Students were so focused on the content and how cute the baby koalas on the page looked that they missed my entire strategy work.

I might say something like this when I set the context for the modeling (see "Before Modeling" for the steps). "I am going to show you one of the ways I figure out new and unfamiliar word meanings. As I read, I stop and look for clues in and around the sentence the word is located in. I might even use the visuals and text features. Please watch how I do this so you can use this strategy in the future when you come across unfamiliar words. Here is how it goes . . ."

ACTION 2: SHOW THE STEPS BY DEMONSTRATING

Once I set the context for what strategy I am going to show readers, I begin the demonstration. When I demonstrate, I break down a skill into steps and then go through each step

> **Before Modeling**
>
> 1. Explain what you are going to show.
>
> 2. Explain why you are showing it, clearly stating the purpose and benefit.

MODEL

in front of the students while I think aloud. The most challenging part for me is being clear on the steps. I plan for this by using the strategy with a text and then slowing myself down and naming each step I took. For example, if I decide the students may benefit from learning a strategy for previewing an informational text before starting to read it, I will take out a few articles and books and do this work myself, without students. The reason I do this work myself across a few different texts is to ensure I am not teaching a strategy that will only work with one text. I always want to make sure what I am modeling is a strategy that students can use with the many different texts in their hands.

Pages from *How Is My Brain Like a Supercomputer?* by Melissa Stewart.

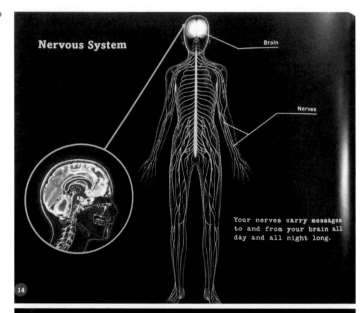

Gravity Goldberg

The next chart shows the difference between strategies that are text specific and those that can be used across texts. Text-specific strategies are limiting because they cannot be replicated across texts and situations by a variety of readers like we have in our classrooms. Instead we can look at the second column of the chart for examples of strategy steps that most students can use when needed in a variety of texts. This column sets students up to choose when they need a strategy and to maintain their ownership of their reading processes. What we show with one particular text can be transferred to other texts and readers.

Text-Specific Strategy	Strategy for Use *Across Texts*
When Previewing 1. Read the heading, Nervous System. 2. Look at the picture of the human body and locate the nerves and brain. 3. Think about what you might learn about the nervous system before you begin reading the words.	**When Previewing** 1. Read the heading. 2. Look closely at the visuals, captions, and labels. 3. Based on the heading and visuals, think about what you might be learning about to get your mind ready to begin reading.
When Monitoring 1. As you read about the brain as a supercomputer, stop when you get to the part that says "6,000,000,000,000." 2. Make sure you understand what this number says. 3. Reread and use clues in the sentence to help you and don't just keep reading on until you figure it out.	**When Monitoring** 1. As you read, make sure you are picturing and understanding the information. 2. When you get to a part that is confusing or does not make sense, stop. 3. Then use all the clues in the sentences around the confusing part, the visuals, and what you know about the topic to clarify what the information means.

Previewing and Monitoring Strategies

MODEL

Once I take the time to figure out the steps of the strategy, I can easily plan the demonstration. First, I choose a text to demonstrate with. I tend to choose a text the students will enjoy and also one that is at an appropriate level and topic. Second, I use sticky notes to mark where I will show the strategy. The photo below shows one example of what these notes look like. They list the steps for me so I can remember the language I want to use when thinking aloud. The same language and steps might end up on a chart so students can not only hear my steps but have a visual to read the steps as well.

After selecting pages from a book that will be used in a demonstration (*How Is My Brain Like a Supercomputer?* by Melissa Stewart), I plan by listing my strategy steps on a sticky note. By writing the exact language I will use in my demonstration, I can consistently and clearly tell and show my reading process. If I can't write the steps on one sticky note, it is an indication that what I am trying to model is too complicated or too wordy. If so, I go back and make it clearer.

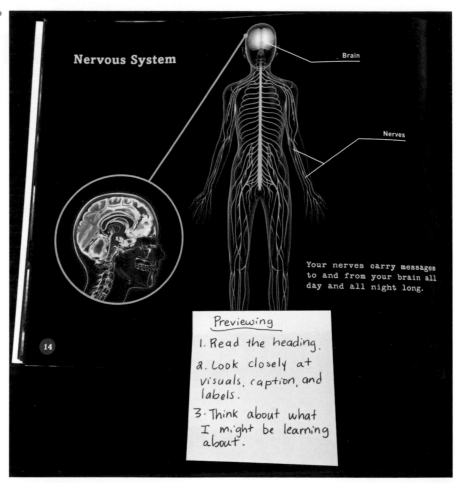

Gravity Goldberg

When I demonstrate, I make sure to follow the steps of the strategy I've already outlined and to narrate and think aloud as I do each step. The demonstration sounds like this:

"I want to preview these pages before reading so my brain will be ready to access all that I already know about this topic and what else I might be learning. I am going to show you one way I preview informational text." (This is the part where I set the context and tell students what strategy I will be showing them and why.)

"First, I am going to read the heading." *I point to the heading and read it aloud as I put one finger up to show this is the first step.* "So it says, Nervous System. Second, I am going to look closely at the visuals." *I put up a second finger as I state this second step.* "Well, this looks like the human body but not the outside. It looks like a series of connected pathways in the body. The label says 'nerves,' so maybe these are the nerves running through the body. And then there is the brain and a zoomed-in picture of the brain with different colors." *I am thinking aloud here so students do not just hear me state the steps of the strategy, but also see me show the work I am doing as I use the strategy. This is my "reading show," and I want to let them see me at work.* "I better read this caption. It says your nerves carry messages to and from your brain all day and all night long. OK, so if I put this all together, this page seems to be showing me nerves and how they are connected and run throughout the whole body and how they are the communicators that carry messages to the brain. Oh, so this is why it is called the nervous system, because the nerves run through the whole body and form a connected system." *I put up my third finger as I explain the final step of the strategy.* "Third, I need to use this information to think about what I might be learning about when I begin reading the words. Well, I think I will learn about nerves and how they carry messages to the brain and throughout the body. I think I will understand more about what the nervous system actually is and does."

In this demonstration example, I made sure to show each step and not just tell it. I also used my fingers as a sort of visual list for students to follow along. Thinking aloud as I showed each step gave students a glimpse into my process and also made it clear that reading strategies take some work. Sometimes when our demonstrations are too rehearsed and too planned out, it can come across to students like the strategy is super easy. They see us move through each step effortlessly, and then when they go back to try it, they get frustrated because it requires much more work and effort than what we modeled. For this reason, I tend to show my work, and sometimes I even explain how much effort it is taking to figure it out. This normalizes effort as an essential part of reading closely and also as something even adults do. I am subtly reinforcing a growth mindset when I show the effort and work I put in. And I am showing I am human, not a perfect reading machine who never encounters challenges.

MODEL

ACTION 3: SUMMARIZING BY NAMING WHAT WAS DONE

After I finish showing students my use of the strategy, I summarize what they just saw by naming what I just did. This may sound redundant, but I find that most students benefit from hearing me name the steps one more time for them, especially after they just saw them. This might be the time I refer to a chart as well. I might say something like this as I point to each step on the chart: "So you just observed me as I previewed an informational text so I could get myself ready to learn about the topic." I recap the what and why for them. Then I restate each step of the process. "I am sure you noticed that first I read the heading. Second, I looked at the visuals, caption, and labels, putting the information together. Third, I thought about what I might be learning about as I read the words, based on what I just looked at closely." I remind students when this may be helpful for them in the future—when they might choose to use this new tool. "When you are reading a new section or new informational text, you might want to use this strategy, to preview before starting to read the words. This strategy can help you so you don't approach a text or topic without background information and ideas about what you might be learning in mind."

I often refer to a chart when I name my strategy steps as a model. I try to match what I write on the chart to what I say when I think aloud in my demonstration. I tend to use quick sketches and visuals along with words on my charts so students have a visual reference. I may even photocopy a page from the book I modeled with, so students remember the context in which they saw the strategy used.

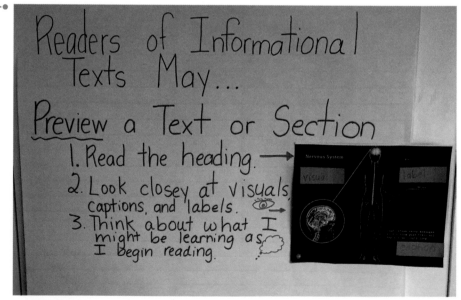

Gravity Goldberg

Being a Model to One Student

Chris and I were collaborating in her seventh-grade classroom during independent reading. We were spending the period conferring with students about their reading work during a unit of study on character relationships and the lessons we can learn from them. This unit was created after we read the standards and thought about the interests of the students in the class. Each seventh-grade reader chose a fiction book and was pursuing a line of thinking around character relationships. Chris and I chose this focus because it was broad enough to offer lots of choices and options for students to think about and connect with, but also narrow enough that readers could have conversations with each other about what they were learning. We also chose this focus because students in seventh grade tend to be learning about relationships in their lives and navigating relationships with their peers, their teachers, their coaches, and their families. We predicted this unit focus would hook these readers, and it really did. On this particular day, students were reading their self-selected books. Chris had spent time conferring with her students on a regular basis and had already been a miner, uncovering what they did as readers, and a mirror, giving growth mindset feedback about their process. She sought me out on this day to work more on being a model to some of her students.

The first student Chris wanted to teach was a young man named Tim. Chris had uncovered that Tim was the type of reader who got lost in the action of the story and seemed to fly through action-packed books without stopping to think too much about what was motivating all of these actions or what he could learn from the characters. She had given him feedback about how he knew what he liked to read and chose books that he could be swept up into and that he finished books every few days and immediately began a new one. She decided he could benefit from teaching around how to think about why characters were making the decisions they did and how it was often influenced by the other characters in the book—that character relationships shaped the action. She was going to model this for Tim.

I observed as Chris became a model for Tim. She sat down next to Tim and began her teaching with the first action—by setting the context and explaining. "Tim, the last time we met, you were showing me how you finished two books in the *City of Ember* series by Jeanne DuPrau. You were excited to start the third book. I noticed that you are flying through this series and really enjoying the books. When I read them, I had the same experience. I was thinking I could teach you one of the ways I use the characters' relationships to understand books even deeper. I am thinking this might add a whole other dimension to your experience as a reader." He nodded as Chris set up the context for her demonstration. She remembered to be an admirer of readers and not a fixer, so she brought her own books with her and took one out to model.

"Tim, I am reading this book called *Escaping the Giant Wave* by Peg Kehret. It is action packed and about a middle school boy who is on vacation when an earthquake hits his hotel area. As I read, I find myself wanting to flip through each page quickly to find out what is going to happen next. What I am going to teach you today is how I first pause when the main character has a decision to make. Next, I think about why the character might be making this choice—what is motivating him? Then I notice how the character's motivation can offer clues about what might happen later in the novel that I can use to make predictions. Let me show you what I mean." Chris stated the steps of the strategy and was about to show the steps.

"Early in Chapter 1, the main character, Kyle, learns his parents, his younger sister, and he are going on vacation together to the Oregon coast. Here on page 6 his mom explains to Kyle that he is old enough to babysit his sister and that they no longer need to hire a babysitter. Kyle asks his mom how much he will be paid for this job, and his mom explains this is just a part of his responsibility as a family member and he doesn't need to be paid. I am noticing that Kyle has a decision to make. He needs to decide how to handle this request to babysit his little sister. So rather than reading on immediately, I am going to pause and think about what might be motivating his decision. Well, it seems like Kyle views babysitting his little sister as a job and that he wants to be paid for the work. It might also be that Kyle wants spending money on his trip and sees this as an opportunity to make some. I guess his need for money and his valuing of his own time and work are motivating him to ask to be paid." Chris was thinking aloud and showing Tim how she thought about the character's decisions.

She went on, "Now that I thought about the character's motivation, I want to use this to predict future events. Since Kyle seems motivated by making money for his trip and wants his work and time to be valued, I think he will continue to babysit his sister while on their vacation only if and when he is compensated. If he is not compensated, I think he will be upset and possibly not do a very good job of watching his little sister." Chris demonstrated the steps of the strategy and was thinking aloud to show her process. Chris worried the importance of this scene might be lost on Tim, so she explained a bit more about why understanding the motivation here early on in the book was helpful.

"While this might not seem like a big decision, it is giving me clues about the characters' motivations and how they may impact decisions in the future. I know from reading the back cover summary that there will be an earthquake later when he is babysitting his sister. So this moment when he has to decide whether he will babysit or not is really important. This will be interesting to think back to when I get to the earthquake scene and how he handles it." Chris finished showing her thinking on the third step of her process.

Chris finished the demonstration by summarizing and naming what she just did again for Tim. "So Tim, I am sure you noticed my steps. First, I paused when the character had a decision to make. Second, I thought about what was motivating his decision. Third, I used his motivation to predict his future actions and decisions." Tim nodded and smiled to acknowledge he did notice those steps.

In this conference, Chris showed Tim a clear strategy that she thought would benefit his deeper reading and study of character relationships. She went on to discuss how and when he might use this strategy in the future. Tim explained that he does tend to focus solely on the main character and he gets caught up in the decisions but doesn't tend to think about what is motivating these decisions. Then he added, "I guess it is just like in life. Like when a person makes a decision, there is always a reason behind it, and if we figure out why they do what they do, we really know them better." Chris replied, "Yeah, that is why we can study character relationships and decisions and learn lessons from them that we can use in our own lives."

Gail has already taken time to be a miner and mirror and really knows this reader. She is modeling a strategy in this reading conference. She chose to model this strategy based on knowing what this reader could benefit from learning next. Notice Gail models in her own notebook that she carries with her when she confers with readers. This ensures she does not take over her students' work.

MODEL

Gravity Goldberg

By setting the context for what she was going to model by **explaining** how the strategy would help him, she set Tim up to learn a strategy. When Chris took out her own book to model, she was **demonstrating** to Tim not only the process, but that she is a reader too and that she can show him what she actually does when she reads. By **naming** what she did after the demonstration, she made sure Tim did not just focus on her book and its plot but also focused on the strategy he could take with him. Sometimes Chris even leaves a sticky note that lists the steps or asks the students to take notes as needed to remember the strategy. At the end, Tim made a connection to when and why he would use this strategy and seemed to understand it as a reading and life tool and not an assignment for the teacher.

Are We Really Modeling?

It can be challenging to know if we are actually modeling and not reverting back to our habitual teacher actions. The chart below shows what modeling is and what it is not. I often use this chart with teachers when we are learning to take on the role of a model as a reference point we can use together. It can be easy to move away from modeling and into something else. This "something else" that is not modeling might sound like assigning, guessing the teacher's thinking, or prompting. These actions are not a part of being a model.

Remember a reading model's job is to *show a process*. It would seem crazy for a chef to stop in the middle of her cooking show to ask the audience, "What temperature should I set the oven?" We are watching her show to learn this very step. If we knew the answer to that question, it would be our show, and we would not need to watch hers. Instead she shows us how she sets the oven to 375 degrees, modeling her steps. We might need to rewatch an episode just like readers might need to see a demonstration a few times. When reflecting on your own modeling, you can consider if you are starring in your own reading show.

Modeling Is	Modeling Is *Not*
☑ Breaking down a skill into steps	☐ Telling students what to do
☑ Showing *how to* do something	☐ Asking for help from students
☑ Thinking aloud as you do the work yourself	☐ Telling what you would do
☑ Showing	☐ Asking questions

Clarifying Modeling Behaviors Chart

Planning to Model for the Whole Class

In whole class minilessons, teachers model strategies for readers and show their process. I recently worked with a group of fifth- and sixth-grade teachers to plan a series of minilessons based on their mining, using data from their classes. We had a discussion about what modeling was and was not and then listed out minilesson topics. As we began the discussion, one teacher, Katie, said, "We can teach a mini-lesson on what point of view is." Another teacher, Grace, said, "Yes, and they really need to know how to identify the point of view of the author and how to interpret bias and also how to validate information." We listed these possible minilesson topics on a piece of chart paper. There seemed to be a clear divide in the list. Some of the topics were focused on what a concept is, and the rest of the list was focused on how to do something. Here at right is an example of our list.

> **Possible Minilesson Topics**
> - What is point of view
> - How to identify point of view
> - What is bias
> - How to identify bias
> - How to validate information

If this list was going to be turned into minilessons that included a clear demonstration of modeling our strategies, it needed to include a strategy that was a how-to. So we sorted this list into the topics that included a how-to and the ones that did not. We really could only model a strategy if it included a how-to. The ones that did not include a how-to, such as "what is point of view" and "what is bias," would not make good minilesson topics because there would not be a strategy to model. Instead we decided to turn the "what is" topics into read aloud lessons where we would read an example and tell the students what the term meant. Since minilessons are not the only instructional component we have available for teaching, we might choose read aloud time to preteach what something is and our minilessons to demonstrate how to do something. When we make this distinction, it helps us avoid turning minilessons into lectures where we stand and explain what concepts are while students passively sit waiting to learn how to do something.

We planned minilessons that included a how-to, and we used the steps I described above. We tried the work ourselves in different articles and named what we did in a series of steps. Then we chose an article to demonstrate from. We used sticky notes to mark where and what we planned to demonstrate. Our plans included a list of minilesson topics and a few articles marked up with notes. As we planned, I was reminded of what Kathy Collins taught me about planning reading instruction. She explains, "When I plan for the work my students will do . . . I always

MODEL

begin by considering what real-life readers would do and what habits of mind they need to use if they were doing a similar kind of reading. For example, when I plan for what I want my students to learn during a character study, I always begin considering what I and other proficient readers might do when we think about the characters in our texts" (Collins, 2008, p. 47).

Preparing to Be a Model

Being a Model
★ Set the context and explain.
★ Show the steps.
★ Summarize and restate steps.

In order to be a model, you do need to be prepared. Chefs don't cook a meal for the first time on their television show. They first create recipes, test them out, and think through the steps. The same can be said for our reading demonstrations. In order to prepare and plan for demonstrations, you might want to take the following steps:

1. Get clear on what readers would benefit from learning. Do your job as a miner first. Make a list of possible topics for demonstrations. These can be for the whole class, small groups, or individuals.

2. Gather a few texts that go with the topic and try the work yourself. Notice what you are doing and list the steps you took.

3. Use sticky notes to mark where you can demonstrate and what language you can use when you think aloud.

4. Remember the actions a model takes and possibly carry a reminder with you when you demonstrate. It might look like the reminder note above.

Modeling, Not Assigning

As a model, I am not trying to get students to be just like me, to be carbon copies, or to be mimics. Instead, when I model, I am showing an example so students have additional ideas of what reading can look like and sound like and possibly add another tool to their box. My expectation is not that students will always and forever follow my "recipe." I do find that the first time a student observes a strategy, he does tend to go off and try it following my steps. This is totally normal. The first few times I make a recipe, I follow it exactly. But over time, students begin to be more creative and flexible with strategies and begin to own them as their own. This may look like a student adapting some of the steps or a student creating her own steps. As this begins to happen, I give growth mindset feedback and go back to being a mirror to my students.

To avoid my modeling coming across as an assignment, I choose my words carefully. I try to avoid phrases like "I need you to go try this now" or "Now you must . . ." Instead I may ask reflective questions like this: "How might you use this strategy in your reading?" or "When do you think this might be useful to you?" I also make it clear to students at the beginning of the year when I begin modeling that my expectation is that they will choose strategies when they need them and not just use them the day I show them.

I tend to end each minilesson by offering students a minute to think about when and if they will use the strategy I just modeled for them. I do this by reviewing charts of previously taught strategies as well as the current one and saying, "Let's take a moment to review the strategies we've learned and our bigger purpose as readers. Now think about where you are in your book, what you are working on, and what strategies you might end up using today. Take a moment to turn to your partners and tell them what choices you might make and why." This final minute of the minilesson reminds students that my modeling is not an assignment and that they are in charge of knowing what they need and choosing it. They own their reading lives.

If students need more support in making choices and not just mimicking what you show them, the next chapter on mentoring will offer more concrete ideas for teaching students how to make choices.

Admiring Trouble

THE "TROUBLE"

After the whole class minilesson when students went off to read on their own, most of the students in the class chose to do exactly what was modeled in the minilesson. These students seemed to want the formula and to stay safe without making choices or taking risks. Even when the minilesson did not really apply to their own reading behaviors or books, students forced the strategy and tried it anyway. It was as if these students forgot what reading was—a process of creating

Students can be models for one another. Two students are teaching their classmates how to set goals for themselves. They refer to a class chart and then model how they set their own goals.

Gravity Goldberg

meaning—and instead saw it as a series of assignments to complete. It seemed like the class was playing a game of Simon Says, but instead it was Teacher Says. Even with the best of intentions, the students were not understanding that the strategies being modeled were a tool to be used when they needed them.

EXAMINING THE "TROUBLE" WITH AN ADMIRING LENS

This all-too-familiar scenario is likely a sign that students have years of experience in school where what was valued was following the directions the teacher gave. The students were taught to turn each day's lesson into an assignment for years, and now that we are asking them to be in charge of their own reading lives and decisions, they may feel unsafe and unsure how to do this. Freedom and choice can be scary too. Rather than tell students to make choices and get frustrated when they do not, we can shift our lens and admire that they do know how to apply and try out strategies in their own books. Just like students were taught how to mimic the teacher and complete someone else's assignments, we can teach students to make choices and give themselves assignments.

WHAT I DID

I ended the reading time a few minutes early, and the class and I gathered for a class meeting and discussion. I took out a piece of chart paper and made a T-chart. I wrote on one side "When I Am in Charge" and on the other side "When Others Are in Charge." I explained to the students that during reading time they are in charge of their own reading. This does not mean they are in charge of everything—they cannot leave class or jeopardize the safety of anyone or choose to break school rules. But they can choose what they want to read, how they read, and what they think about, talk about, and write about on most days. I asked every student to take out two sticky notes and to think about how they behave and the actions they take when they are in charge (in any aspect of their life). Students began to jot phrases on the first note. Then I asked students to think about their behaviors and actions when someone else is in charge. Again, they began to write. This seemed relatively easy for most students. I did notice a few were sitting with blank sticky notes, so I did a quick model using a think aloud. "I notice that when I am in charge when it is dinnertime, I pick things I like to eat. I jotted down the words *pick what I like* on the sticky note." Those few who were not writing began to. The T-chart on the next page shows what we did and what some students wrote.

After the students wrote their sticky notes, we began sharing what we wrote. A student would read what she wrote and then explain it. After that, she would go up and stick it on the chart. Not every student shared that day, but we shared about three or four for each side. Then we looked at the notes and reflected on what it means to be in charge. I asked the students to turn to a partner and explain what it would look like, sound like, and feel like if they were in charge of their own reading. Then I asked the students to consider and discuss what actions and behaviors they would take on when they were in charge of their own reading. I scribed what they said, and we created a list of behaviors that included making choices, being interested, and thinking about what they need.

MODEL

When I Am in Charge	When Others Are in Charge
I pick what I like.	I do just enough to get by.
I think about what I want to do.	I don't always care how I do.
I choose what I need.	I do whatever I am told.

In-Charge T-Chart

WHAT I LEARNED

Students in school might not be used to having ownership and might need some time to really think, reflect, and discuss what this means. Having students think about the places in their lives where they are in charge helped us have a concrete set of actions we could take in reading where they were less used to being in charge. These charts also became a landmark in the classroom where we could go back together and check in to see how ownership was going. It still took time and patience and reflection, but students did eventually begin to make choices and be more engaged as independent readers.

Conclusion

We can choose to be a model for our students once we have identified what they would benefit from learning. Remember that, when we are modeling, we are starring in our own reading show, and we are showing students how we read and use strategies. The three main actions we can take when we are models are as follows:

1. Set the context by explaining what we will be modeling and why.

2. Show students the steps of the strategy by demonstrating and narrating what we do.

3. Summarize what we just showed students by restating each step.

Finally, when we are models, we are not playing Simon Says and trying to get our students to do exactly what we just did. We are offering examples, showing steps, and encouraging application when needed.

In Chapter Eight, I will explain the role of the mentor and how we can guide students to try new ways of reading. This means we can support students as they make choices and begin trying new or complicated strategies in their books. We move from being the star of the show who is front and center to the one on the sidelines offering ideas and prompting actions.

Andrew Levine Photography

CHAPTER EIGHT

Be a Mentor
Guiding Students to Try New Ways of Reading

Shortly after my first soccer season began at Boston College, it became clear that my coach was extremely experienced and intense. However, she was also very pregnant. Unlike some of my previous soccer coaches, who were mostly men, she could no longer step on the field and play with us during practice. She had to restrict her coaching to being on the sidelines, observing us practice, and then giving detailed directions for how we could lift our level of play. I did not realize the benefits of this coaching style until the following soccer season.

A year later, we found ourselves with a new soccer coach. She was fresh out of college and an incredibly talented soccer player in her own right. In fact, she was a better player than most of us. Her coaching style often included her stepping on the field in practice and playing with us. She ran up and down the field, giving us beautiful passes and helping us score lots of goals. The only problem was she was not allowed to play on the field with us during our games. While we were excellent in practice with her contributions from the field, we were less successful with her on the sidelines. We were so used to her doing much of the work for us

Andrew Levine Photography

that we were not as prepared to do it on our own. The best coaches know when to guide from the sidelines and when they need to step onto the field. They know when to be models but also when to be mentors.

Being a Mentor

After spending time modeling my strategies for readers, I realize they will likely need support in actually applying and trying out each strategy in their own reading. When I show students what I do, it can look easy enough, but when readers go off to try the strategy on their own, they may realize it is much more challenging than they originally believed. When this happens, I take on the role of a mentor, guiding and coaching readers to try new strategies once we have already determined it can benefit them. In this chapter, I use the terms *mentoring* and *coaching* interchangeably because the best mentors I know act as coaches. As a mentor, I try to be on the sidelines of a student's reading. This means I observe, call out "plays" or prompts, and guide the student through tricky parts. This does not mean I do the work for the reader. I don't get on the field or in the book. Remember, I carry my own books with me as a model to demonstrate from so that, when I am finished demonstrating, I can mentor the reader in her own book. Modeling happens in the teacher's book, and mentoring happens in the student's book.

I find it helpful to compare what the mentor does and does not do, and the chart below shows what coaching as a mentor entails.

Mentoring Is	Mentoring Is *Not*
☑ Guided practice through each step of a process	☐ Correcting miscues or errors
☑ Prompting students with a reminder of a strategy they can try	☐ Asking questions with a "right answer"
☑ Nonverbal signals or reminders	☐ Asking leading questions
☑ *Telling*	☐ Using overly general directions

Clarifying What Mentoring Is

As you recall from the previous chapter, being a model means showing your process to students. Being a mentor, on the other hand, means telling your students what they can do. When I am acting as a mentor, I imagine myself as a coach on the sidelines. My job is to guide the readers through each step of a process just like a soccer coach guides players through each step of a corner kick play. There are five qualities I consider when being a sideline coach who sets up readers to try new strategies. Even though I am on the sideline, I am not passive—I am doing the work of a mentor. I guide students through each step of the strategy, give clear prompts, and try to do less and less over time.

Break Down Strategies Into Steps

My soccer coach did not say, "Score a goal!" as she mentored from the sideline. She did not say this because that is simply the end result we were hoping for. Instead, she broke down what it would take for us to score a goal into smaller steps we could perform while ultimately trying our best to score the goal. She would direct, "Pick your head up. Now look for who is open. Pass the ball hard right in front of the net." These were steps I could follow one at a time (albeit to varying degrees of success). As a reading mentor, I also try to break down my directions into steps so readers can focus on how to perform the strategy. Early in my teaching career, I would simply say, "Now find the main idea," without showing students the steps for how to do it. This was the equivalent of saying, "Now score a goal," and I know they needed more guidance and support.

NAME ONE STEP AT A TIME

When students are practicing a new strategy, I try to observe them as they work and name only one step at a time. When mentoring a fourth grader in how to infer a main idea in a nonfiction article recently, I used the following steps in my guidance.

"As you are reading, pause when you come to a word or phrase that is repeated," I said, and waited for the reader to do this. "This might be the main topic of the section.

"Now think about why this word or phrase is repeated." The reader stopped and thought about this. He told me his thinking.

MENTOR

"Put this together," I suggested. "Ask yourself, what is the author telling us about this topic?" As the reader began to think about this, I pointed to his reading notebook.

"Write this main idea in your notes about the topic so you don't forget." Taking notes, in this case, was something the student already knew how to do and did not require directions or guidance for.

In the above example, I broke down a strategy into each step and told the reader what he could do one step at a time. If I had told him all those steps and then walked away, he might have been overwhelmed and confused. As a mentor, I often guide students through the process from beginning to end.

TELLING, NOT QUESTIONING

When I am guiding readers through the steps of a strategy, I am telling them what to do. This could sound contrary to the idea that we want reader ownership. But let's take a step back for a moment. I only act as a mentor once I have worked *with* students to determine what they are already doing and what they could benefit from adding to their tool kit of strategies. As a mentor, I have already done my work as a miner, mirror, and model. I can only mentor readers once I have uncovered what they are already doing well, given growth mindset feedback, and demonstrated an additional strategy they could add to their current processes. By the time I am choosing to be a mentor, the students are ready to be guided through a new strategy.

If I have not done my work as a miner, I end up trying to include it in my mentoring, and it sounds like a bunch of questions. Notice I did not ask the student to tell me the steps in the previous example. I told him the steps. I did not say, "What should you do first?" If I were to ask that question, I would be assessing whether or not the student knew the first step of the strategy. Assessment is the work of the miner. By asking that question, I would be trying to get the reader to guess the first step. The questions I ask in a mentoring session are ones the readers can ask themselves, not ones for me. I know that when I go into questioning mode instead of telling mode when being a mentor, I often leave frustrated because the reader cannot guess my thinking. Take a look at the next chart and notice the difference between mentoring by telling the actions and questioning that elicits the steps from the readers.

Telling	Questioning
• Look at the heading.	• What can you look at?
• Break that word down into parts.	• What can you do with that word?
• Pause when the character shares his internal thinking.	• Where can you pause?
Directs the reader with actions to take	*Tries to elicit the steps from the reader*
Guides the reader with something to try	*Assumes the reader knows what to do*

Telling and Questioning Comparison Chart

Notice that the telling column includes actions the reader can take. This is because they are steps to try right away as readers. The questioning column, on the other hand, gives students something to think about, but they are left unsure what to actually do. If they can answer a question correctly, they already knew what to do and likely did not need us there mentoring them. If they cannot answer our question, then they need us to tell them anyway. I recently explained it this way to a teacher I was collaborating with. When I know what I want the students to try out and be able to do, I just tell them. I don't play "guess my thinking." If I have a genuine question about what the reader is doing, I go back to my role as a miner and uncover her process.

FOCUS ON WHAT TO DO

When I was trying to get the soccer ball past an opponent defender, my coach did not say, "Don't give the ball away." She also did not say, "Don't let them get past you." When coaches focus on what not to do, it can get in our heads and end up focusing our attention on what we don't want to happen. I once heard a speaker say that, when we tell ourselves not to do something or to avoid something, our brain actually does not remember the *not*. That means we are reinforcing the behavior we do not want. Instead of focusing on what not to do, we can prompt readers by focusing on what to do. If I notice myself putting all my attention on the negative outcome or what I don't want to happen, I try to simply switch it around. The examples in the chart on the next page show how I switch my focus from what not to do into a positive action: steps to do.

MENTOR

Avoid These Types of Prompts	Switch to These Types of Prompts
☐ Don't keep reading when it doesn't make sense.	☑ Stop when it doesn't make sense and try rereading.
☐ Don't just retell the last part of a short story.	☑ Retell the entire short story, including the beginning, middle, and end.
☐ Don't pay attention to tiny, insignificant facts.	☑ Focus on the main ideas and facts that support them.

Comparing Prompts

If I find myself stuck in the negative prompts, I pause before I speak to the reader and picture the action that will help the reader and focus on that. Notice how the first word in each "what not to do" prompt is *don't*. Right away, when I hear the word *don't*, I get a little anxious because my attention is on what I want to avoid. Now notice how the prompts that focus on what to do all start with an action word—something I can go try to do right away as a reader. I feel more clear and confident when my attention is on what I can actually do. Think about it in your own life. If your roommate or partner says, "Don't forget to take out the garbage," you might be so focused on the forgetting you actually do forget. If, on the other hand, the request sounds like this—"Remember to take out the garbage"—you are focused on remembering.

KEEP PROMPTS CLEAR

The directions I tell students while they are trying a new strategy are prompts that are meant to be short and clear. If I have to use paragraphs of talking to explain what to do, it is unlikely the students will remember them after I leave or even be able to follow them in the moment. I try to be efficient with my word choice, avoid jargon, and be direct. Notice the difference between the long, paragraph-style approach to prompts and the short and clear approach in the next chart. I can keep it short and clear if I have already modeled the strategy for the readers. Since they have already seen me use the strategy and explain when I choose to use it, they don't need that reminder in the middle of trying it out themselves.

Short and Clear Prompt	Long Paragraph-Style Prompt
Notice the dialogue. Identify who is talking. Make your voice match the character.	When you are reading dialogue, make sure to find out who is talking. Look for the quotation marks. The quotation marks show you the exact words the character is saying. The words after the quotation marks are who said the words. You will want to change your voice when you read so that it sounds like the character is actually talking. So if you are reading a young girl character's dialogue, you can make your voice sound like a young girl would sound.

Short and Long Prompt Examples

One of the reasons I keep my prompts short and clear is that I want students to remember and use these steps again on their own. I hope my voice ends up being their own voice in their head the next time they are reading dialogue. When I was a child and teenager, my grandfather, Papa Joe, would repeat phrases of guidance to me. He would say things like "Be sharper than a marble" when I needed to make a big choice. Since he repeated this clear guidance to me as an adult, I still carry those words with me. What we say to readers can leave a lasting impression. If we keep our prompts short, clear, and direct, they may repeat those same steps to themselves when needed.

OVER TIME, DO LESS

My mentoring is not always the same for every student or for every teaching time. If I have already spent time mentoring students by guiding them through each step with lots of prompting, I may choose to do a bit less the next time they try to use the strategy. If I am always offering lots of support, readers can become dependent on me to take them through every step every time. After a few times of being told to "pick my head up and look in the center of the field" by my soccer coach, she no longer needed to tell me all the steps. If I did need guidance, she might simply say, "Center!" That single word was enough to remind me of

MENTOR

the step. Later she might not even say a word; she might just point to the center of the field. As a reading mentor, I try to do less over time as well.

We can think of doing less as gradually releasing more responsibility of remembering the steps to the readers so they are doing more as we do less. In this way, they begin to develop ownership of the strategy. To this day, when I play co-ed soccer, I look to the center of the field because I have ownership of that play. The visual below shows a continuum of more to less support when it comes to mentoring readers. It also shows how the students develop more ownership when less support is offered over time.

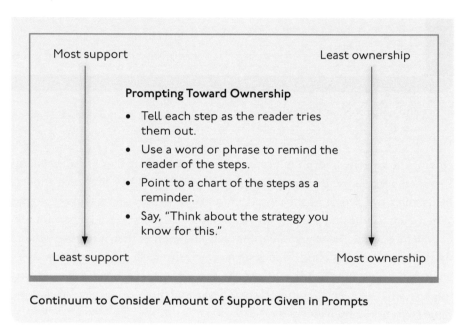

Most support

Least ownership

Prompting Toward Ownership

- Tell each step as the reader tries them out.
- Use a word or phrase to remind the reader of the steps.
- Point to a chart of the steps as a reminder.
- Say, "Think about the strategy you know for this."

Least support

Most ownership

Continuum to Consider Amount of Support Given in Prompts

As a mentor, I am guiding students to try out new strategies and also observing their degree of success. My ultimate goal is for the new and prompted strategy to become a part of the reader's process that he uses when needed. If I want readers to choose strategies, I need to offer less support over time so they are ready to make that choice.

Mentoring a Small Group of Readers

Having already spent time modeling a strategy to a small group of third graders, their teacher, Stacy, wanted to spend time mentoring these readers to try the strategy themselves in their own books. Stacy modeled how to figure out long, multisyllable words by breaking them into parts and thinking about what would make sense. She chose to teach this strategy because these three students tended to either skip long new words or say a nonsense word and keep on reading even if it did not make sense. On this particular day, she was meeting with the three students to coach them through trying the strategy. She had already explained to them what she was going to coach them on and why.

Stacy decided to first mentor these readers on a common text from the class read aloud book, and then she would mentor them as individual readers in their own books. She held up the read aloud book, *The Most Beautiful Place in the World* by Ann Cameron, and turned to page 35. The class had already read this chapter, and Stacy was referring back to the part with a long, multisyllable word. "Remember this part where the main character, Juan, sneaks back into his mom's house to sleep with her even though he was supposed to be living with

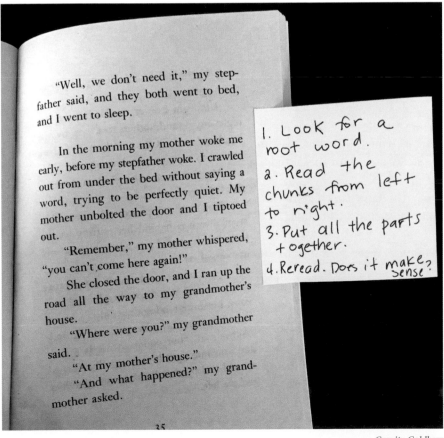

Read aloud excerpt (*The Most Beautiful Place in the World* by Ann Cameron) for student practice and mentoring.

MENTOR

Gravity Goldberg

his grandmother?" The group of students nodded. She showed the page to the students with a reminder of the steps they were already shown about how to solve a long word.

When Mentoring
- Name one step at a time.
- Be direct and tell.
- Focus on what to do.
- Keep it simple.
- Do less over time.

"We are going to read this part together, and when we come to the long, unfamiliar word, we are going to stop and point to it." Stacy handed out a copy of the page to each student in the group, and they followed along as she read. When she got to the word *unbolted*, she stopped and did not say the word. Instead she said, "Hmmm. This is a long and unfamiliar word." The readers all pointed to the word. Stacy began mentoring them to try to solve the word with the strategy she had already modeled. She began prompting them to use the steps of the strategy. With each prompt, she tried to use the five qualities of mentoring.

"Look closely to see if there is a root word. Point to it." Stacy's students pointed to the word *bolt*. Stacy pointed to the minichart of the strategy steps she had made on a sticky note (see the photo on the page 163).

"Look for chunks and say those parts quietly as you move from left to right through the whole word." Stacy was naming each step one at a time and was being clear and direct. She was not asking the students what to do or look for. She was telling them and coaching them to try each step as she also pointed to the sticky note chart that listed the steps.

"Put all of those parts together and make it sound right." She listened as students said, "Un-bolt-ed. Unbolted."

"Now let's make sure it makes sense. Reread the sentence trying that word." Students reread and then said, "Yep."

Since the students were successful in using the strategy on this common text, Stacy decided to mentor the readers in their own independent books next. She told the students to take out their own books and begin reading. When they came to a long and unfamiliar word, they could use this same strategy to try to solve it. The students picked up their books and began reading. She did not artificially tell them to look for an unfamiliar word. If she were to do that, it would send the message to students that the goal was to use the strategy. The goal of this lesson was not to use the strategy. Stacy wanted her students to have a tool to use when they came across long words they did not recognize; her goal was to make sure they could figure them out. While this strategy was about word solving, it was really about comprehension. If students do not read words accurately and skip them or say nonsense words, this interferes with understanding and comprehension. Each student began reading his or her book as usual, making sure to use a variety of strategies as needed to make meaning of the text. As students came across longer unfamiliar words, Stacy offered them prompts to solve them. She used the same language she did the first time she coached them, but this time she did not show the sticky note chart. Stacy simply told the students each step as they practiced the strategy on a word in their independent book.

I noticed that all three students were able to practice and apply the strategy in that seven-minute small group lesson. Because Stacy had already done the work of being a miner, she knew this was a strategy the students would benefit from learning and using. This is why it was not forced, but applicable right away. If we

This reader is engaged in reading and applying the strategy she was just coached to try. After we are mentors, we still need to step back and give readers space to keep practicing on their own. We continue to coach as needed and may step in at a subsequent conference to re-coach and shore up the use of the strategy.

Gravity Goldberg

MENTOR

have to force the mentoring of a strategy, the students likely don't need it just yet, and it is not the best time or context to prompt them to use it. At the end of the lesson, Stacy reminded the students to keep using this strategy as needed whenever they were reading and came across long and unfamiliar words. But she also reminded students that it would not always work. Like any strategy, it may take more than one attempt to use it well.

The next time Stacy worked with these three students, she did not give them as much support as she did during the initial mentoring lesson. Instead, when she was working with each student during a one-on-one conference, she simply said, "Remember what you can use to solve that word. Roots and chunks." That simple reminder was enough for them to recall the steps and use them. Stacy hoped that over time the students would use the strategy without any prompting at all. She would keep working with them until they owned the strategy, offering them a little bit less each time.

Mentoring the Whole Class During a Read Aloud

Whole class read alouds provide opportunities to mentor the entire class in using a reading strategy. Because I am reading aloud the text, I can choose one text that may even be above the reading level of many students, but one that offers opportunities for deep thinking and discussion. While reading aloud the picture book *Fly Away Home* by Eve Bunting, I used the opportunity to mentor the class in how to identify and interpret symbolism. This is a rather complex skill, so the read aloud is an accessible first step in mentoring students. I had already modeled one way I interpreted a symbol in the book *The Other Side* by Jacqueline Woodson. During this read aloud, I wanted to help readers begin to do this work themselves. Since this was a complicated concept, I was tempted to "get on the field" or in the book and do the work for the students. Instead I pulled out a class chart (like the one at left) that listed the steps of the strategy I already had modeled and began reading the story and supporting their use of the strategy.

Interpreting Symbols

1. Look for an object that creates a vivid image in your mind.

2. Think about what this object means in the context of this passage.

3. Think about what else this object means in life outside of this passage.

4. Ask yourself, "What could this object represent in this part?"

In this picture book, a young homeless boy and his father are living in an airport. One day, the boy finds a bird that appears to be trapped in the airport. I began reading the book and stopped toward the end when the boy wants the bird to fly free of the airport. I looked at the class. "I am noticing there may be a symbol here we can interpret. Remember, when we interpret symbols, it helps us understand a story beyond a literal 'what happened' level." I knew the students already knew what a symbol was, so I was able to begin prompting their interpretation. "Let's notice an object that keeps coming up in this story—an object you can really picture or is on almost every page's illustration. Jot the name of the object on top of the page in your notebook." I expected each student to name the bird or the windows in the hangar because they were an obvious choice, but it would be fine if they chose a different object. I pointed to the chart of steps and noticed it was as helpful to me while I prompted them as it likely was to the students who needed the visual.

"Think about what the object means in this part of this story. What does this object literally mean? You can jot a few words to remember your thinking." I paused and gave the students a few moments to think and jot. Once many students seemed finished jotting, I gave the next prompt. "Now think about what the object means outside of this context—in the world. How do others think about and view this object? Add more thinking to your notebook." A few students appeared to struggle at this point. I decided to give them a few more moments, and when a handful of students still did not jot anything down, I decided not to do the work for them, but I did refer back to the modeling I had done previously with *The Other Side*. "Remember how I thought about how fences are dividers and are used to show people and animals where to stay and where to go?" This reminder seemed to help them get thinking and jotting.

Finally, I prompted, "Think about what this object could represent in this part of the story. Put all your thinking together. What does this object stand for that the author is not explicitly stating?" I observed as students reread their jottings and then added a bit more. I asked the students to turn to a partner and explain what object they thought was a symbol and how they interpreted it. Readers turned to one another and showed their notebooks and explained their ideas. For example, one student explained that the windows symbolized hope for what could happen in the future. Another student explained that the windows were made of glass and since the bird kept flying into them they represented the hidden barriers the boy and the bird faced. After their discussions, I finished reading the rest of the book and gave students the opportunity to add to or revise their interpretations as needed.

MENTOR

This beginning experience with interpreting symbolism was just the start to a series of mentoring sessions so students could eventually begin to interpret symbols on their own when needed in their own books. In subsequent experiences, I would simply point to the chart or give just a few key word reminders when we did this work in other read aloud examples. I would likely begin to use more complicated and less obvious examples over time so students would continue to progress with the skill.

Admiring "Trouble"

THE "TROUBLE"

As Stacy continued to work with the readers in her classroom, a small group of them seemed to sit passively and wait to be told each step of the strategy. They did a wonderful job of following the steps but did not apply strategies on their own. They only seemed to use new strategies when told to do so. Stacy did end every mentoring experience by saying something like this: "From now on, you can continue to use these steps on your own when they are needed." Even with this reminder, these few students appeared either unwilling or unable to try on their own. Stacy and I discussed this observation, and we wondered if it was not that they were unwilling or unable but perhaps that they did not understand when to use a strategy. They did have the tool, but they might be unsure when to pull it out and use it.

EXAMINING THE "TROUBLE" WITH AN ADMIRING LENS

If we stuck with our "unwilling and unable" lens, we would likely have been frustrated and given up on these students. Luckily, we supported each other in taking on an admiring lens. We decided the *what* and the *how to* seemed clear to the students but the *when* was unclear. Instead of focusing more on the steps of the strategy, we focused on helping students understand when the strategy applied.

WHAT WE DID

Stacy and I discussed our options, and we called the students over to the small group area for a conversation and an experience focused on *when* to choose a strategy. We had spent five minutes the day before choosing and photographing four different objects and placed them near four blank sticky notes. Stacy asked the students to notice that one column consisted of tools that students use. The other column of sticky notes was blank because we were going to discuss when we would choose to use each tool. We chose these four tools because we were confident they were quite familiar for students.

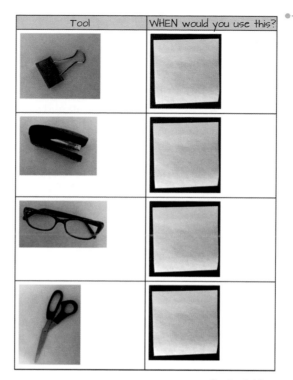

Tool	WHEN would you use this?

Gravity Goldberg

This is an activity for mentoring students about how to match a tool with a purpose. I use this to teach *when* to apply a strategy.

As we discussed the first tool, a large paper clip, the students said they would choose to use it *when* they had several pages they wanted to keep together. We jotted that on the sticky note next to the clip. We proceeded in the same way by discussing when we would choose to use a stapler. When we got to the last two tools, the glasses and scissors, we asked the students to think about when they would use them, and they made their own quick notes on a sticky note. They all had virtually the same things written down for the scissors, but the glasses were interesting. One student wrote and explained he would choose to use this tool when he needed to see objects that were far away because he was nearsighted. Another student explained that she would use the tool when she was reading and writing and doing schoolwork because she needed them to help her see up close. The other students explained they would not use this tool because they did not need glasses to see well. The glasses were a tool that we discussed a bit more because it helped the readers realize that tools were not used at exactly the same time for each reader or in exactly the same way.

We segued from discussing the four tools and when we would use them to discussing reading strategies and when we would choose to use them. Stacy

MENTOR

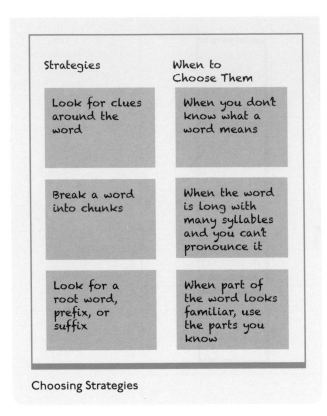

Strategies	When to Choose Them
Look for clues around the word	When you don't know what a word means
Break a word into chunks	When the word is long with many syllables and you can't pronounce it
Look for a root word, prefix, or suffix	When part of the word looks familiar, use the parts you know

Choosing Strategies

explained, "Just like we can choose when we need to use a stapler, we can choose when to use a word attack strategy or a character inference strategy. We choose strategies when they will likely help us. And we might all make different choices based on what we need and on what our books require of us." She took out a stack of more sticky notes and asked the students to help her create a chart of reading strategies and when they might choose to use them. For this experience, she focused solely on word attack strategies since that was the area she was mentoring them with at the current time, but she did explain that this was true for all strategies and not just word attack.

Stacy asked each student to write down on a sticky note one strategy they sometimes used when trying to read challenging and unfamiliar words. The students each wrote down a strategy in their own words. Then Stacy collected and lined these up on a piece of small chart paper, as shown above. The final part included the students collectively thinking about when they might choose each strategy and then adding these sticky notes next to the strategy. Together they made a chart they could refer back to, but they also had an experience building confidence to know they can decide when they need a tool.

WHAT I LEARNED

Even though we often try to set students up to own the strategies we teach them, they may still struggle with figuring out when the strategies apply. Some students may not trust themselves enough to make choices about when a strategy could be used. If we help them build confidence with everyday school tools such as scissors and staplers, students can begin to feel ready to make bigger choices about strategy use. When we meet students where they are and then build from there, we can support the development of confidence. I also learned the importance of including the *when* in all of my teaching so students understand when to make a choice. Finally, I was reminded how powerful an admiring lens is for both the teachers and the students. If we hadn't taken on an admiring lens, we might have written these students off as risk avoiders or resistant to independence, and we might not have found a way to help them make choices. Admiring doesn't just feel good but also helps us meet our students where they are and support their continued growth and development.

Conclusion

When we choose to be mentors to our students, we are guiding them to try a new strategy we have already identified they would benefit from using. The role of mentor tends to come after the work of being a miner, mirror, and model. That way, we are choosing to mentor readers in a strategy with which they are familiar.

Think about the type of reading coach you tend to be. Are you a "sideline guide" or an "on the field" coach who takes over much of the work? If you find yourself in your students' books doing much of the work for them, you can be a mentor by

- naming one step at a time that they can try,
- directing them with action-focused prompts,
- focusing on what to do,
- keeping it clear, and
- doing a bit less over time.

In Chapter Nine, I will help you think about five types of lessons you can teach so the students in your class begin to take on an admiring lens too. I explain fourteen lessons you can try with your students so everyone in the class has ownership and is an admirer.

MENTOR

Teaching Students Strategies for How to Be Admirers

CHAPTER NINE

Andrew Levine Photography

I learned to swim as an adult. As a soccer player and runner, I was always athletic, but swimming was never something I found time to learn. This all changed the year my friend Renee and I signed up for our first triathlon where we would be swimming a mile in the Hudson River. We joined a gym with a pool, bought bathing suits and goggles, and signed up for a lesson. The first time we waded into the shallow end and began swimming across the length of the pool, I realized my version of the doggy paddle was not going to get me very far. I looked around and noticed how everyone else, including the 7-year-olds in the lane next to me, knew how to swim freestyle, putting their heads in the water, breathing left to right, and actually moving gracefully across the pool. Renee was much more comfortable than I was and seemed to make it across a few times before needing a break. I told myself that day, "I am a terrible swimmer. I should never have signed up for this race. What was I thinking?"

Luckily, the next time I entered the pool, I was with a swim coach, Maria. She watched me attempt to get across the pool, barely sticking my head in the water and gasping for air each time I did. Maria called us over to the edge and said,

"Great job! Since you already know how to float, we can begin working on breathing." I was shocked. "I could already float?" I wondered to myself. She went on to teach us breathing techniques and drills we could practice to learn proper form. Maria started each lesson by observing us swim across the pool (something I did eventually learn to do) and naming what we already were doing well and then building the drills and sessions around what we needed to learn next. Even more surprising than my ability to learn to swim was the way my thinking about my swimming began to change. I began to notice what I was getting better at. I began to tell my friends I was learning to swim. I even went as far as asking my mom if she wanted to come to the race to see us dive into the Hudson River. I began to admire my own ability as a swimmer the more I worked with Maria. Since this first season as a triathlete, Renee and I have gone on to complete three Ironman races and completed 2.4-mile swims in the Ohio River and the Hudson River. With hard work, I did eventually become a proficient swimmer.

When I think back to my time learning how to swim and my continual work as a swimmer, I notice five lessons I have learned along the way. First, I learned the language of swimming and how to talk about what I was doing while I swam. I learned words like *pull* and *drag* and *bilateral breathing*. Second, I learned to stop comparing myself to the other swimmers and to set reasonable goals for myself. It began with being able to swim a whole lap using freestyle. Third, I learned that what I told myself about my swimming ability and the mindset I carried really impacted how fast I progressed and how often I practiced. Fourth, I learned how to take the feedback Maria gave me and use it to improve my stroke. Finally, I learned to ask for support when I needed it. For example, before the big race, I asked for help with how to "sight" in the open water when there are no lanes to keep you on a straight course. Each of these five lessons helped me learn to be a stronger swimmer and also to actually enjoy those laps in the pool.

Teach readers how to
- Talk about their reading process
- Set goals for themselves
- Reflect on their mindset
- Give each other feedback
- Ask for support

I start with this story because my goal for students is not simply that we teach them to read well but also that they begin to identify as readers and begin to admire their reading process the way I learned to admire my swimming. The previous chapters explained how to take on new roles as reading teachers, admiring what students do, and creating an environment where true ownership can occur. This chapter leaves us with five skills you can teach students so they can begin to admire their own process and develop ownership of it. These lessons are similar to what I learned as a swimmer. The following is my top five skills to help readers develop an admiring lens themselves. The remainder of the chapter describes specific lessons you can teach across the year.

How to Talk About Your Reading Process

When readers are being taught to describe and talk about their reading process, they need a little background knowledge to get started. First, readers need to know what a process is. I teach what a process is in a few ways. I tend to start teaching concepts about what something is by bringing students' attention to an area they already know a lot about such as a process for lining up at the end of the day to leave or a process for choosing what to wear that day. By beginning with what they already know, they can focus on the process—the how-to and the steps of what they tend to do.

These readers often meet at the end of Reading Workshop to share their reading processes and to teach one another how they are reading. Students learn from one another's descriptions and get more ideas for how they might read.

Gravity Goldberg

Create a T-chart with the class and on the left side label it "What I Do as a Reader," and the right side can be labeled "My Process (What Are My Steps?)." I begin modeling one reading skill I use and my process for doing it. Then I add this to the T-chart. Once I am done modeling, I ask students to pay attention that day during independent reading to what they are doing and how they are doing it so we can discuss it at the end of the period. I explain that we can learn from each other by getting to know and then describing what we do as readers.

What I Do as a Reader	My Process (What Are My Steps?)
try to get lost in the story and make it come alive	make movies in my mind, picturing the characters, the setting, and the action

Class T-Chart of Reading Processes

At the end of the reading time, after I have worked with students one-on-one or in small groups as a miner, mirror, and mentor, we meet back as a whole class in the meeting area. I ask them to turn to a partner and try to name what they did and describe their process. As students talk to each other, I listen so I can choose who I think should share with the entire class today. I ask a few students to share with the class and be the model. We add their process to our T-chart. This becomes a chart that can grow over time and be added to and referred back to as students become more aware of what they do as readers.

Lesson 2
Using a Visual to Show the Process

Some students seem to be able to name their steps of the process easily while others simply shrug when asked about it. Even when I work with adults who are proficient readers, it can be challenging to describe our process because we just do it without thinking about what we are doing most of the time. Another way I approach this idea of being able to talk about our reading process is to ask students to think about what they do as readers as a visual and to sketch what it looks like and feels like. I tell them not to overthink this and that there is not one right way to do it. Again, since this is a new experience for most, I typically model what one of my visuals looks like. The image below is one I often use to show my process.

I explain that sometimes it feels like a big wide spiral that gets smaller and smaller and more clear and focused as I read, think, jot, and talk. For me, it starts with my purpose for reading the text, and then I end up reading, thinking, jotting, and talking (not necessarily in that order) over and over again until I finish the book and I come back to my purpose. A student once said it looks like the layers of an onion, and that seems to work too.

One visual I use to show my reading process like a spiral.

Gravity Goldberg

After modeling, I ask students to read and pay attention to what visual might represent what their process was that day. At first, the students tend to be analyzing what would be the right visual. I explain there is no right one. I say, "If your reading process was a picture, what would it look like?" This is not a fluffy activity, but another way to help readers explain and talk about their process. A few examples of what readers have created include riding waves, a staircase to a magic door, and a cupcake.

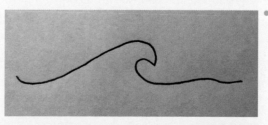

One reader's visual to show the reading process like a wave.

Gravity Goldberg

One reader's visual to show the reading process like a staircase to a magic door.

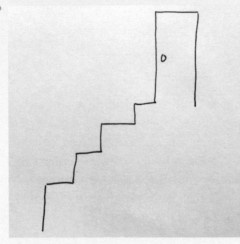

Gravity Goldberg

One reader's visual to show the reading process like a cupcake.

Gravity Goldberg

While I was working with teachers in Los Angeles, one reader explained his process was like riding waves in the ocean. He described it as paddling out to the wave and anticipating what it would be like, then seeing the wave and riding it until it flattened out and you were back to where you started. The other readers in the class were fascinated by his visual and description. Many explained that riding a wave was a lot like reading action-packed books.

Another reader, in a different class, drew a staircase to a magic door. She explained that reading sometimes felt like a slow walk up stairs until you come to a door and you have to reach out and turn the handle. As a reader, you just don't know what is going to be on the other side. It feels like magic, and all you know is that you will be somewhere else from where the stairs started and it was worth the climb. Wow! Sometimes reading does feel like a steep climb to a magic place.

A third example is a reader who drew a cupcake with sprinkles and frosting. He explained that he likes it when reading is like a cupcake because it means there are a lot of sprinkles and frosting, which are like interesting details that get you hooked. Then as you eat further and get to the cake, it might not be as sweet as the frosting, but it is still good and also what the cupcake actually is. It is like you find what it really is, and it is not what the frosting made it look like.

These three readers were able to talk about their reading process when I allowed them to use a visual and a metaphor to explain. We posted these visuals around our T-chart in the classroom and referred back to them as ways of talking about our process. Readers would sometimes say, "Today feels like riding the waves," or "I am getting past the frosting," to describe their process.

Lesson 3
Learning the Language of Reading

Just like I needed to learn the language of swimming, it can help readers to learn the language of reading. One way to do this is to go back to our class T-chart of what we do as readers and our reading process. We can reread it and use sticky notes to label the reading terms that the descriptions refer to. This is not to correct students' work but to add to it. This is a way we teach Tier 3, domain-specific vocabulary that teaches readers ways of using the words of reading. We can ensure we are all speaking the same language when we talk about our processes.

What I Do as a Reader	My Process What Are My Steps?
try to get lost in the story and make it come alive	make movies in my mind, picturing the characters, the setting, and the action envisioning

Class T-Chart of Reading Processes With Labels

When readers talk about their process, they can refer back to our chart, their own visual, and the sticky notes with our specific reading language. Whether it is in a reading conference, a partnership, or a book club conversation, readers are talking not just about their books but about how they go about reading them—their process.

How to Set Goals for Yourself as a Reader

A second skill I teach is how to set goals for yourself as a reader. By signing up for my race, I had set a goal for myself as an aspiring swimmer, and it helped keep me motivated across those difficult training sessions. I suggest you teach students how to set short-term goals as well as long-term goals. This is because short-term goals, when met, help us gain confidence and stay motivated. I did not just have the goal of completing my race but had smaller ones along the way such as my goal to swim a lap using freestyle at first.

If students are new to setting their own goals as readers, it can be helpful to begin with a short class list of goals where students can select from the list. Some teachers make a big poster-sized chart that lists the goals, and the students write their name on a sticky note and place it next to the goal. This way, the goals are identified by the teacher, but the students select the one they feel ready to work toward. It might look like the chart below for a character study. The students' names are on sticky notes, and they can choose which goal to work toward and when they are ready to move their sticky note to a new goal. This is a first step in goal setting because it limits student choice to which goal and when to choose it but does not teach them how to create an original goal quite yet.

Character goal chart for students to work from.

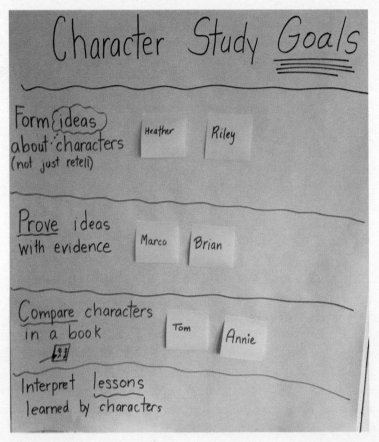

Gravity Goldberg

Lesson 5
Creating Goals From Categories

Once you have taught students how to choose goals from a class list and they are able to select goals with confidence, you can move to the next level. This next level is when readers choose their own goals from a category. This is just like when I set a goal for myself in terms of how far I wanted to be able to swim without taking a break—a stamina goal. I also had goals for pace and speed, but these were different.

As a novice swimmer, most of my goals were focused on stamina and speed because they were so tangible and I was not knowledgeable enough about swimming to set more nuanced goals. This may also be the case for student readers. At first, students might set goals focused on fluency and getting fast at reading because these are tangible goals. We can guide students to envision other types of goals that may help them as readers even more. This is especially important as more and more readers seem to read fast to get through a book and miss out on enjoying the experience of reading. The chart pictured here shows how one teacher, Pam, helped students identify goals from categories. Pam set the categories at the start of the year, and the readers wrote their own goals for the category they selected. Many readers chose fluency and stamina goals, but as the year progressed, these categories were replaced by more comprehension-based goals.

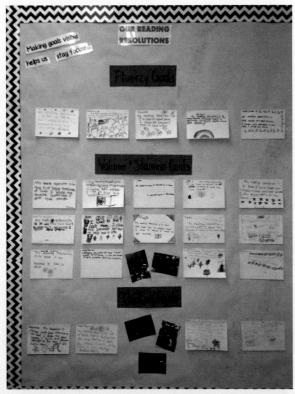

Third graders' goals at the start of the school year.

Pam Koutrakos

Lesson 6
Create Personalized Goals

Eventually, when students are really owning their reading process, they may begin to create their own personalized goals. These tend to stem from reflecting and discussing with the teacher what big-picture goals the reader wants to achieve. One seventh-grade teacher I work with sits with each student quarterly to have a goal-setting conference. In the conference, the student sets the agenda and leads the discussion. The student spends time looking through artifacts from the quarter such as a list of books read, entries in the reading notebook, previous goals, and notes. Then the reader writes a personalized goal and what it might take to reach it in her reading notebook. These goals may include reading more challenging books, learning to read between the lines more and understand what else might be going on besides the action, finishing more books and not abandoning them, or trying new genres and authors. There is no wrong goal.

How to Reflect on Your Mindset

Students work together to set self-directed reading goals. They have learned these goals can focus on reading behaviors such as reading silently, reading habits such as stopping at unfamiliar vocabulary to use strategies to figure out the meaning of a word, or thinking processes such as considering characters' motivations. Students often choose goals based on the conversations they have with one another and the feedback they receive.

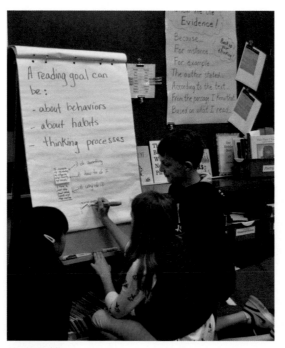

Gravity Goldberg

A third skill I teach is what a mindset is and how to reflect on yours. Dweck's (2007) work on growth and fixed mindset along with Achor's (2010) work on beliefs can be simplified and explained to students so they can begin to reflect on not just how they read but how they think about themselves as readers. It wasn't until I began to view myself as capable of learning to swim and calling myself a swimmer that I really saw a huge improvement in my ability and my confidence. The same is true for readers.

Lesson 7
Using Read Alouds to Teach Mindset

I teach what a mindset is by reading aloud some picture books that show examples of it. Some of my favorite books for teaching mindset include *Ish* by Peter H. Reynolds, *Beautiful Oops!* by Barney Saltzberg, and *The Most Magnificent Thing* by Ashley Spires. After I read these aloud, we discuss the characters' mindsets or beliefs about themselves and their abilities. We identify examples from the text that show a growth and fixed mindset. If I have a document camera to project, we can mark places in the book with a sticky note. Or students can write examples of the mindset on sticky notes, and we can sort them on a mindset chart.

Pam models her thinking about the characters in this read aloud. She shows the class how she considers the mindset the character is taking on.

Gravity Goldberg

Lesson 8
Analyzing Characters' Mindset

Once we have done these short read alouds, we can begin to analyze the characters' mindsets in our books. Most teachers teach how to analyze a character's traits, feelings, or motivations. We can also teach readers to analyze the character's mindset. I can model how I do this in a class read aloud book one day or in a minilesson another day. Readers can figure out what mindset the character is holding by paying attention to what types of thoughts the character has and how the character handles challenges. Readers can mark places in their independent books that show the character's mindset and discuss this with a partner. By noticing the character's mindset, they are more deeply understanding what mindset really is.

After the minilesson identifying the character's mindset, you may want to teach a lesson on how the mindset is impacting the character. Create a list of questions to consider, such as these:

- Why does the character have this mindset?
- How does the character act when he or she has this mindset?
- How is this mindset impacting the character's actions and decisions?
- What is the character losing or gaining as a result of this mindset?

Focusing on the characters first, before themselves, can help students feel safer about this topic. It can be vulnerable to look at your own mindset, but looking first at characters' mindsets puts the lens out there at first instead of on us.

Lesson 9
Identifying Our Own
Mindset as Readers

After discussing and analyzing characters' mindsets, many students naturally begin reflecting on their own mindsets. One student recently asked, "Can you have one mindset in one area and a different one in another area?" We went on to have a class discussion about how sometimes there is an area where we hold a growth mindset; for example, I did as a runner. I always believed I could continue to get faster and stronger the more I trained. But, as a novice swimmer, I held a fixed mindset at first, believing I would never be a swimmer (until my coach Maria helped me change that limiting belief). Now I realize I can teach students that our mindsets can change and develop differently in different areas.

I ask students to open their reading notebooks to a blank page and honestly think about what mindset they might be holding about themselves as readers. I may ask, "Right now, what do you believe about your ability as a reader?" Then I give them a few minutes to write. I may follow up by asking, "What mindset do you think these beliefs support?" Then I give them a few more minutes to write. I can typically tell by scanning the faces of the students as they write how they are feeling about their mindset. I end by explaining that mindsets can and do change all the time. If we have a fixed mindset about ourselves as readers right now, that does not mean we will always have that mindset. I say, "The good news is this: Our mindsets can be changed, so if you don't like what you just noticed about yours, you get to change it, and I can help you."

After reading Shawn Achor's book *The Happiness Advantage* (2010), I learned many concrete tools for changing our belief system to one that is more positive and growth mindset based. I adapted his strategies for the reading classroom. The following list contains quick and easy ways to teach readers to develop a growth mindset. You can do this with the entire class on a regular basis because consistency is important when changing a mindset. Ideally, these strategies become habits.

The teacher and student work together to reflect on the student's reading goal. These goals are written on sticky notes on a class chart. The student can take the sticky note off the chart and bring it to a reading conference for discussion and support.

Gravity Goldberg

- End the reading period with partners sharing one positive thing they learned that day about themselves as readers.
- Regularly ask students to write down three positive things about themselves as readers. Make sure they are specific, such as "I can break up big words into parts and figure them out" or "I can infer the character's traits."
- Celebrate challenges and the tenacity it takes to work through them. Once a week, ask a student to share a challenge he faced and what he learned from it. You can be cheesy and call it "Tenacity Tuesday."
- Ask readers to write down a fixed mindset belief they hold about themselves as readers on a single sheet of paper. Create a letting-go ceremony where they can choose to let these beliefs go by shredding them, tearing them up, or putting them in the compost bin at your school. By literally letting go of these beliefs, they can begin to replace them with growth mindset beliefs.

How to Give Each Other Feedback

Readers get feedback not just from their teachers but also from each other. This can be formal feedback in a peer conference or more informal feedback in a quick turn and talk conversation. By learning to give growth mindset feedback to their classmates, readers are also developing an admiring lens. My swimming partner Renee and I did not just say to each other "Good job" at the end of our training sessions. Renee would say, "I noticed your arms were even and your pull was propelling you through the water." This feedback was specific and helpful. By giving me this feedback, Renee was also learning to be more aware of her own swim stroke.

Lesson 11
Listen, Look, and Label
(Without Opinions)

Students seem to give each other positive feedback regularly such as "Great job!" or "Way to go!" As you recall from Chapter Six, this type of feedback is too general to be that helpful. You can teach students to give each other the 3 Ls of feedback. They can first listen to each other. This seems obvious, but many students I work with are so busy thinking about what they want to share that they are not actually listening to one another. I teach them to listen and make sure they understand what their classmate is saying. This may require asking clarifying questions if needed. The second L is for looking. Teach students to look at each other's notebook entry, sticky note, or part in their book. It helps to actually look at the part the reader is talking about. The third L is for labeling what they notice. Spend a minute teaching the difference between a label that states what is there and one that states an opinion. This label is not an opinion; it is a statement of what is there. You can use a visual with labels to show what you mean. The label states what the reader did.

I use this image to show an opinion versus a label when I am teaching students how to give feedback. Students can use the image to compare the feedback they are giving to the examples shown.

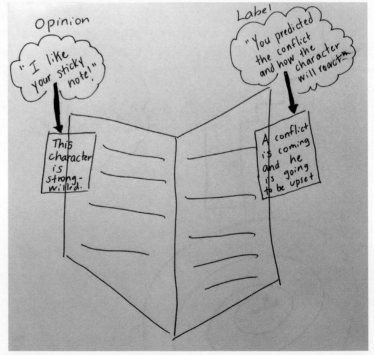

Gravity Goldberg

Lesson 12
Discuss the Outcome

After teaching partners to listen, look, and label when giving feedback to one another, you can teach them to discuss the outcome of what they did as readers. After giving feedback such as "You predicted the conflict and how the character would react," the partner can follow up by asking, "What happened when you did this?" or "How did this help you?" By asking an outcome-based follow-up question, readers are helping each other think about how their process is working for them. In this way, partners are acting as miners for each other and not just mirrors. Over time, the readers may end up asking themselves the same questions their partners are asking them, and it can become a natural part of their reflection process.

How to Ask for Support

When I realized I needed more support as a swimmer, I would ask Maria or Renee for help. Early on I would ask, "Can you help me swim better?" Maria would respond by asking me what I specifically needed. I learned to ask for support differently. I would say, "Now that I know how to breathe on the right side, I want some help learning how to breathe on the left side too." Maria would sometimes get in the water and show me a drill. Sometimes she would have me watch Renee do it, and sometimes she would email me a link to a video to watch. Maria taught me how to ask for support and where to find it. Readers will also need support, and we can teach them how to ask for it and where to find it.

Gravity Goldberg

These two readers are meeting to offer each other feedback. They are practicing what they were taught by their teacher and trying to label without offering their opinions. Students often explain how much they benefit from peer feedback.

Lesson 13
Getting Clear About What You Need

When I sit with readers, they often ask me, "Can you help me be a better reader?" Or a reader will come tap me on the shoulder and ask, "Can you tell me what this word means?" These requests show how some readers know it is OK to ask for support. Other readers I work with do not ask for support and have the "I better go it alone" attitude. I teach students that it is normal and often necessary to seek support as readers. I clarify that this does not mean that every time they come to a difficulty, they ask a teacher to solve it for them. We can teach students how to get clear about what they need support with.

You can show students that even as an adult reader, there are times you need support from others. Give an example of a time you needed help. Then show them what you do and don't mean by being clear on what you need. Perhaps model what you don't mean by being clear first. For example, I explained that I went to my friend and asked her, "Can you help me understand this article about gardening since you are an avid gardener?" She wanted to help me but did not know where to start since I just asked for help understanding. It was a very vague request.

Getting Clear on What You Need Support With

1. Describe what you are doing as a reader.

2. Explain what is challenging for you.

3. Ask for specific help with this challenge.

After showing what you don't mean, you can model what you do mean by being clear. I could use the same example but this time ask it this way: "I am reading this article on gardening, and it keeps mentioning pruning. I am having trouble understanding this concept of pruning and picturing what it looks like. Can you explain pruning to me or help me find some pictures that would help me understand?" You could go on to explain that in the second example you named what you were trying to do, what was challenging for you, and what you would like help specifically with. You could chart this, as shown here, so students really understood.

Once you model how you get clear on what you need support with, ask students to do this work prior to asking you or a classmate for help.

Lesson 14
Choosing Where to Get Support

Once students are clear on what they need support with, they can begin to choose where to get that support. For many students, that support is almost always us as the teachers. While there are certainly times when we can support them, we also want to teach readers how to seek support without involving the teacher too. You can teach a minilesson where you show students after you get clear on what you need support with how you list possible places where you could get help before choosing where to go. If I were to model further with my gardening article example, I might show them my list of possible places I could get help with understanding the concept of pruning and picturing what it looks like. My list might include the following:

- Do a Google Images search.
- Use an online reference to look up the word.
- Find another article about the topic to get more information.
- Ask a friend who is an expert on the topic.

After modeling making the list, I would show them how I choose where to go first. I tend to model the places that do not involve others first. From then on, when students approach you to ask for help, you can ask them to explain where they have sought it out already.

Knowing when to ask for help is an important part of admiring and owning our own reading lives. We just might want to be careful we are not setting students up to be dependent on others to solve their problems or challenges for them. By teaching them to get clear on what support they need and then really considering where they might go to find that support, we are teaching a process for seeking support. When students care enough about what they are doing to want support, they are invested, engaged, and showing they own the learning.

Conclusion

When we teach readers to be admirers, they begin to wonder about and study their own reading process. From this admiring place, they can begin to take ownership, develop confidence, and self-identify as readers. These five skills can be taught and revisited throughout the year to support students in developing an admiring lens:

- Talk about their reading process
- Set goals for themselves
- Reflect on their mindset
- Give each other feedback
- Ask for support

There is no magic order for teaching these five skills or the lessons that accompany them. Follow your students' lead and use what you've learned about how to admire the readers in your classroom.

In the final chapter, I offer seven entry points for beginning to admire readers. When taking on shifts in roles, lenses, classroom spaces, and feedback practices, we may feel quite vulnerable. Chapter Ten offers specific ideas for how you can embrace the uncertainty that comes with change and a few tools to help you begin.

Andrew Levine Photography

CHAPTER TEN

Embracing Curiosity

Entry Points for Getting Started

Shifting our practices often feels incredibly vulnerable. When we take on new roles—miner, mirror, model, and mentor—we may be filled with uncertainty and apprehension. *What if I am not great at modeling? What if my colleagues won't shift with me? What if someone realizes I don't know how to give growth mindset feedback?* Brene Brown (2012), who studies vulnerability, asks, "What's worth doing, even if I fail?" (p. 42). While I know you cannot fail at being a miner or a mentor, it can leave us questioning when it gets messy and the shift becomes challenging. Brown asks this question because her work seeks to help people be courageous and live a connected and fulfilling life. In essence, I wrote this book so every teacher feels encouraged to be courageous and connected to their students and their work, so that in return they inspire their students to do the same. Brown (2012) describes this sort of vulnerability and courage combination: "We must dare to show up and let ourselves be seen . . . This is daring greatly" (p. 2).

Any kind of change can feel daring and quite vulnerable. Brown explains that when we are vulnerable, we learn to trust, and when we trust people, we are connected and able to show up ready to share all we have to offer. As teachers,

Andrew Levine Photography

we are modeling not just our mindsets and our reading strategies, but also our willingness to be vulnerable and trust. As teachers, we need students to trust us, and we need to trust them. Trust is at the heart of an admiring lens.

In her research with leaders from various sectors including CEOs, managers, teachers, and parents, Brown finds that being vulnerable is an essential element of being an effective leader. She explains how one leader's shift came when she realized "that getting people to engage and take ownership wasn't about the 'telling' but about letting them come into an idea in a purpose-led way, and that her job was creating the space for others to perform" (Brown, 2012, p. 209).

In this chapter, I offer a few entry points for getting started as an admirer (see "Becoming an Admirer"). Since there is no single way to admire, any entry point can be the right one for you. I recommend finding someone you can trust and be vulnerable with, so you can take on these shifts in practice together. I offer entry points as places to begin shifting into an admirer. You may want to begin by shifting your roles. Choose a role to begin with and take it on. Or you may want to begin by shifting your lenses. Consider the current lenses you use as a reading teacher and how much attention is put on you instead of the readers in the class. A third option is to begin by shifting the classroom spaces. Sometimes,

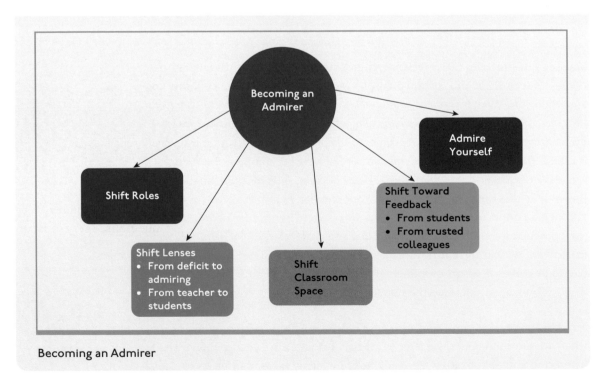

Becoming an Admirer

when we physically change our environment, we can begin to see differently and act differently. A fourth option is to start with shifting feedback practices. Begin asking your colleagues and your students for their observations and ask them to be mirrors to you. No matter where you choose to begin, you can become an admirer of readers.

Entry Point I: Shift Roles

While all four roles work in tandem, it might be more manageable to take on one role at a time when you are making shifts. Think about which of the 4 *Ms* you want to work on first or which one is most closely related to your current roles and students' roles. Study the chapter that explains the role and work with a colleague to take on some of the suggested practices. Remember that none of these four roles is about following a script or fitting yourself in a checkbox. You might want to use the following chart to start a conversation with your colleagues about which roles to take on first. You can ask yourself the reflection questions, review the main actions and practices of each role, and consider which one makes sense to start with for you and your students.

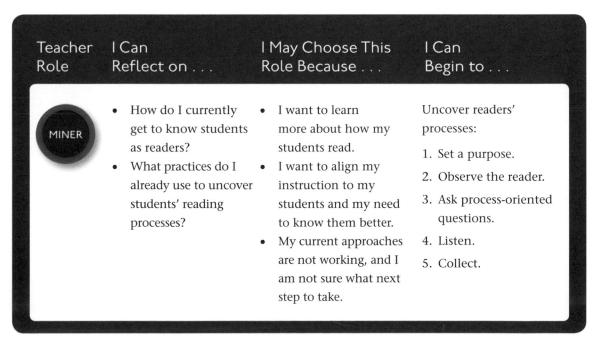

Teacher Role	I Can Reflect on . . .	I May Choose This Role Because . . .	I Can Begin to . . .
MINER	• How do I currently get to know students as readers? • What practices do I already use to uncover students' reading processes?	• I want to learn more about how my students read. • I want to align my instruction to my students and my need to know them better. • My current approaches are not working, and I am not sure what next step to take.	Uncover readers' processes: 1. Set a purpose. 2. Observe the reader. 3. Ask process-oriented questions. 4. Listen. 5. Collect.

(Continued)

(Continued)

Teacher Role	I Can Reflect on . . .	I May Choose This Role Because . . .	I Can Begin to . . .
MIRROR	• What types of feedback do I currently offer students? • How do students respond to my feedback? • What types of mindsets do my students hold about themselves as readers?	• Students do not typically use the feedback I offer. • I am having trouble finding times and ways to give students feedback as readers. • I end up giving similar feedback to every student.	Offer feedback with these qualities: • Be specific. • Name what is. • Focus on the process. • Make sure it can transfer. • Take ourselves out of it.
MODEL	• When do students see my authentic reading strategies? • How do I show students I am a fellow reader? • Am I showing and not just telling about my reading process?	• Students seem unsure or in need of strategies to use as readers. • Students are confused about what strategies to choose when. • Students ask lots of questions about how to do something.	Show readers what I do: • Set the context. • Show the steps. • Summarize and restate the steps.
MENTOR	• How am I guiding students to try new strategies? • How am I supporting students with strategies that transfer? • Where can I be doing less so students can do more?	• Students rarely try out strategies that have already been modeled. • Students ask for lots of help during independent reading experiences. • Students express lack of confidence to try new strategies.	Guide students to try new ways of reading: • Name one step at a time. • Direct with action-focused prompts. • Focus on what to do. • Keep it simple. • Do a bit less over time.

Choosing Which Role to Take on First

Once you have decided which role you want to focus on first, you can reread that chapter and highlight the next steps you want to take. It helps to not get too focused on perfecting any single role before moving onto the next. I still continue to develop and refine my practices within each role, and if I stayed focused on just one for too long, I might end up frustrated. Instead I suggest you take on one role for a few weeks and then move on to the next. Let each role accumulate until all four are being approximated. Then give yourself permission to develop over time. Maintain a growth mindset with yourself as a miner, mirror, model, and mentor.

Entry Point 2: Shift Lenses
From Deficit to Admiring

Another entry point into becoming an admirer is to reflect on the lenses you currently use when approaching the readers in your classroom (see the chart, "Using an Admiring Lens," on the next page). You can begin this process by examining the current beliefs you hold about your students and the roles you tend to take on. For example, make a list of your beliefs about students and consider the practices that grow out of these beliefs, how you talk to the readers in your class, what you say about them to your colleagues, and what you expect from readers. All of us fall into deficit lens thinking at times, and by recognizing it, we can take steps to shift away from it. A focus on what students *cannot do* and *do not do* may indicate a deficit lens.

Rereading the first three chapters of this book and considering how ownership is developed, why it is important, and what an admiring lens means may be helpful to sharpen your focus. Recall the tax auditors who developed their ability to find errors because they looked for them everywhere (Chapter Three). If you have developed the ability to find perceived deficits everywhere, you can shift and develop skill in looking for strengths.

Entry Point 3: Shift Your Focus
From the Teacher to Students

Perhaps you want to shift your lens from a teacher focus to attention on students. Recall in Chapter One how I realized we were admiring the teacher, Gail, but forgetting to admire the students. The Student-Focused Reading Checklist (Appendix A) may be helpful in shifting the lens on the students. If this student-focused checklist

I Can Reflect on . . .	If I Tend to . . .	I Can Begin to . . .
What do I focus on when I approach readers?	• Notice the mistakes a reader made • Focus on what they are not able to do	• Refocus on what the reader is doing and approximating • Observe, discuss, and take notes about strategies the reader *is* using
What kinds of feedback do I offer readers?	• Spend time fixing mistakes and correcting readers • Tell students only what they need to do next that they are not currently doing	• Name the reader's process in a neutral way like a mirror • Point out growth to students and discuss how the reader is developing
How well do I know each reader?	• Use narrow assessment data to know readers • Assume a reader's level tells the story of who she is	• Admire the reader and study her with wonder and curiosity • Become a miner and uncover who this reader really is

Using an Admiring Lens

does not match your intentions, create your own with a colleague. By focusing on the students, we begin to create the context for reader ownership.

Entry Point 4: Shift Classroom Spaces

Look back at Chapter Four and envision what a classroom space focused on admiring looks like. Look at your classroom space. Are you inspired to make any changes? Consider the following questions when looking at your classroom space:

• Have I designed the space to make room for whole group, small group, and independent reading?

- How have I created spaces so students feel ownership of their reading lives? Examples might include reading nooks, a student-organized classroom library, student-written book reviews, and self-selected use of materials.
- Do I have ways to showcase and work toward goals in our classroom space?
- Have I included ways that guide and respond to students on our classroom wall space?
- Does student work show the individual choices of readers?

By making choices about how the classroom space is organized, you can begin to create space that shifts the focus to admiring readers. Perhaps one of the visuals from Chapter Four will inspire you to create a mindset chart with your students. Consider seeking student input about how to organize the classroom library. Showcase student work that shows growth and learning and not just perfection. You might even want to photograph your classroom in a "before" photo shoot by documenting what it looks like today. Then spend some time daydreaming about what you wish it looked like. Sketch your vision. Finally, document the changes you and the students make along the way by taking "after" photographs. Keep the space a work in progress and use a growth mindset, knowing it can and will continue to evolve with your students.

Students who are in charge of their reading feel empowered, energized, and proud. These readers wanted to show their energy for reading.

Gravity Goldberg

Entry Point 5: Shift Toward Feedback From Students

Don't forget to enlist support from your students. Whenever I am feeling like I need some feedback on how the classroom is working, I ask the students. I call a class meeting or meet with readers one-on-one to hear their perspectives. You might reread one of the visuals from Chapter Two for ideas, "A Continuum: How We Might Shift Our Instruction Toward Ownership" (see also Appendix B). This figure invites ways to reflect with your students on the roles they take on and how much of the time you assign, monitor, and manage versus the time your students spend in these roles. Ask students for their experiences and reflections on the balance you provide and how much ownership they feel they have as readers. Engage them in helping you shift so they feel more in charge of their own reading lives.

The list below offers ideas for the types of questions you may ask your students. You can ask these in a whole class conversation, in small group conversations, or one-on-one in conferences. Some teachers even send out a survey and ask for student feedback a few times a year.

- What aspect of reading do you feel works best for you?
- What do you wish there was more of during reading time?
- Are there areas in which you would like to have more choice? Which ones and why?
- What is most important to you as a reader? Can the classroom do more to support you with this?
- If you could change one thing about our reading class, what would it be? Why?

Questions That Elicit Feedback From Students

Entry Point 6: Shift Toward Feedback From Trusted Colleagues

Find a fellow teacher or literacy coach you trust and ask for feedback. This is a vulnerable move for many of us. I recall the first time I asked my colleague Malini, who was also teaching third grade, to come observe in my classroom and offer me feedback. I wanted her help because I knew something was off and I respected and valued her opinions. As you recall, this is also what Gail did in the opening chapter of this book. Malini and I sat at lunch that day, and she acted as a mirror, naming what she saw the students and me doing. I felt safe and trusted because she named what was working well for my students. We began to make it a regular practice to sit in on each other's rooms during reading time and help each other afterward by being mirrors, giving each other growth mindset feedback.

Brown (2012) explains, "Trust is a product of vulnerability that grows over time and requires work, attention, and full engagement. Trust isn't a grand gesture—it's a growing marble collection" (p. 53). Creating some intentions around asking for feedback can be helpful in building trust. I have found it helpful to name what I am hoping my colleagues will look for in my room and teaching practices. I find it most helpful when I make it about my students and use the qualities of being a mirror that I explain in Chapter Six. Approach each other with an admiring lens and look for what is going well that can be built upon. It may help to use a guiding question or focus to ground the feedback time as productive and helpful. For example, if you are not sure if you are offering students feedback that is fostering a growth mindset, ask for that to be the focus. Finally, take turns. After Malini came into my room, I went into hers. We were able to learn with and from one another.

Entry Point 7: Admire Yourself

We all can begin by admiring ourselves. Study your own process and mindsets as a reader and use this as your starting-off point with your students. Offer yourself the kind of ownership you want to offer students.

This means you can approach yourself as an admirer with these beliefs in mind:

- My teaching of reading is worthy of study and to be regarded with wonder.
- My teaching of reading has its own process that may look different than others.
- My teaching of reading is based on purposeful choices I can make.
- My teaching stems from ownership of my own teaching and reading lives.

Just as we admire readers, we can learn to appreciate those qualities that make us thoughtful and inspired teachers. By reflecting on the intentional choices we make and the teaching practices that shape our days, we can balance vulnerability with growing confidence and greater willingness to take risks on behalf of our students.

Appendix A

Student-Focused Reading Checklist

Category	Student-Focused Observations
Classroom environment	☐ Students refer to charts and choose when and how to use them.
	☐ Students can select from libraries that reflect their levels and interests.
	☐ Students use spaces for whole group, small group, and individual work.
	☐ Students use materials independently and choose them when needed.
Student engagement	☐ Students read for the entire independent reading time.
	☐ Students regularly collaborate in partnerships or book clubs.
	☐ Students think, discuss, and articulate their learning.
	☐ Students work through challenges and confidently choose strategies to use when needed.
Individualization	☐ Students regularly participate in either conferences or small group work.
	☐ Students' unique strengths and needs are used in conference decisions.
	☐ Students are focused and independent.
	☐ Students choose their own goals and self-assess their progress.
Independence and transfer	☐ Students transfer teaching points to novel experiences.
	☐ Students use strategies several days or even months after they were first taught.
	☐ Students can explain their goals, strengths, and next steps as a reader.
	☐ Students do not look for the teacher to solve problems or answer questions.
	☐ Students can explain what they are doing and why.

Copyright © 2016 by Corwin. All rights reserved. Reprinted from *Mindsets and Moves: Strategies That Help Readers Take Charge* by Gravity Goldberg. Thousand Oaks, CA: Corwin, www.corwin.com. Reproduction authorized only for the local school site or nonprofit organization that has purchased this book.

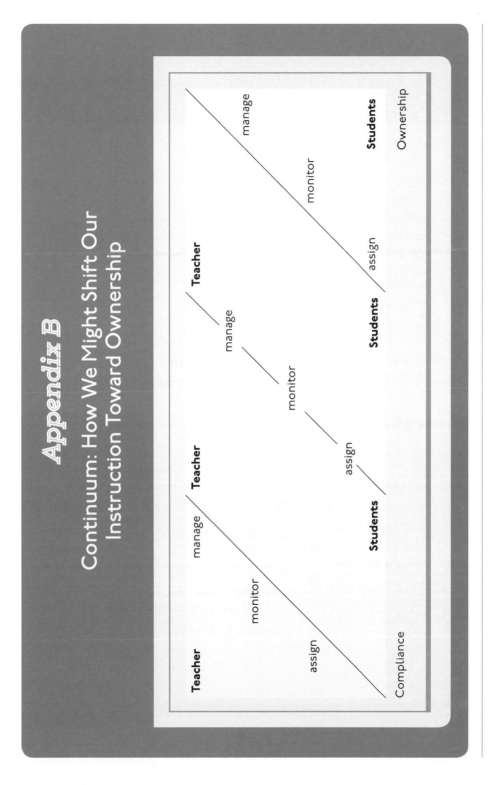

Appendix B

Continuum: How We Might Shift Our Instruction Toward Ownership

Teacher

assign

monitor

manage

Students

Compliance

Teacher

assign

monitor

manage

Students

Teacher

assign

monitor

manage

Students

Ownership

Copyright © 2016 by Corwin. All rights reserved. Reprinted from *Mindsets and Moves: Strategies That Help Readers Take Charge* by Gravity Goldberg. Thousand Oaks, CA: Corwin, www.corwin.com. Reproduction authorized only for the local school site or nonprofit organization that has purchased this book.

Appendix C

Chart of Balanced Literacy Reading Components

Component	Description	Teachers	Students
Interactive read aloud	Teacher reads aloud a text and models thinking by focusing on comprehension strategies and encouraging discussions.	1. Model comprehension strategies 2. Prompt students to practice the strategies (often with a partner)	1. Listen and observe 2. Practice a comprehension strategy in writing or by discussing it with a partner
Shared reading	Teacher uses an enlarged text, and both the students and the teacher collaboratively read, discuss, and analyze the text.	1. Model strategies for comprehension, fluency, or word work 2. Ask students to join in on the work and practice the strategies 3. Study what the author did and use the text as a mentor text	1. Observe and follow along 2. Practice the strategies in writing or by discussing them with a partner
Reading workshop	A brief 7- to 10-minute minilesson is followed by a large chunk of independent reading time for students, then partner talk, and then a whole class share at the end.	1. Teach a reading strategy 2. Have conferences with individual students and small groups 3. Facilitate a share and conclusion at the end	1. Listen during the minilesson 2. Read independently and make choices about how they read and their purposes for reading 3. Teach their classmates by sharing at the end or having discussions

Copyright © 2016 by Corwin. All rights reserved. Reprinted from *Mindsets and Moves: Strategies That Help Readers Take Charge* by Gravity Goldberg. Thousand Oaks, CA: Corwin, www.corwin.com. Reproduction authorized only for the local school site or nonprofit organization that has purchased this book.

Be a Miner

MINER

MIRROR

MODEL

MENTOR

1. Set a purpose.

2. Observe the reader.

3. Ask process-oriented
   questions.

4. Listen.

5. Collect.

Copyright © 2016 by Corwin. All rights reserved. Reprinted from *Mindsets and Moves: Strategies That Help Readers Take Charge* by Gravity Goldberg. Thousand Oaks, CA: Corwin, www.corwin.com. Reproduction authorized only for the local school site or nonprofit organization that has purchased this book.

Be a Mirror

1. Be specific.

2. Name what is.

3. Focus on the process.

4. Make sure it can transfer.

5. Take yourself out of it.

Copyright © 2016 by Corwin. All rights reserved. Reprinted from *Mindsets and Moves: Strategies That Help Readers Take Charge* by Gravity Goldberg. Thousand Oaks, CA: Corwin, www.corwin.com. Reproduction authorized only for the local school site or nonprofit organization that has purchased this book.

Be a Model

1. Set the context.

2. Show the steps.

3. Summarize and restate the steps.

MINER

MIRROR

MODEL

MENTOR

Copyright © 2016 by Corwin. All rights reserved. Reprinted from *Mindsets and Moves: Strategies That Help Readers Take Charge* by Gravity Goldberg. Thousand Oaks, CA: Corwin, www.corwin.com. Reproduction authorized only for the local school site or nonprofit organization that has purchased this book.

Be a Mentor

1. Name one step at a time.
2. Direct with action-focused prompts.
3. Focus on what to do.
4. Keep it simple.
5. Do a bit less over time.

MINER

MIRROR

MODEL

MENTOR

Copyright © 2016 by Corwin. All rights reserved. Reprinted from *Mindsets and Moves: Strategies That Help Readers Take Charge* by Gravity Goldberg. Thousand Oaks, CA: Corwin, www.corwin.com. Reproduction authorized only for the local school site or nonprofit organization that has purchased this book.

References

Achor, S. (2010). *The happiness advantage: The seven principles of positive psychology that fuel success and performance at work*. New York, NY: Random House.

Admire. (n.d.). *Dictionary.com Unabridged*. Retrieved from http://dictionary.reference.com/browse/admire

Allington, R. (2012). *What really matters for struggling readers: Designing research-based programs* (3rd ed.). Boston, MA: Pearson.

Anderson, C. (2005). *Assessing writers*. Portsmouth, NH: Heinemann.

Barnhouse, D. (2014). *Readers front and center: Helping all students engage with complex texts*. Portland, ME: Stenhouse.

Barnhouse, D., & Vinton, V. (2012). *What readers really do: Teaching the process of meaning making*. Portsmouth, NH: Heinemann.

Blackwell, L. S., Trzesniewski, K. H., & Dweck, C. S. (2007). Implicit theories of intelligence predict achievement across an adolescent transition: A longitudinal study and an intervention. *Child Development, 78*(1), 246–263.

Blau, S. (2003). Performative literacy: The habits of mind of highly literate readers. *Voices From the Middle, 10*, 18–22.

Bomer, K. (2010). *Hidden gems: Naming and teaching from the brilliance in every student's writing*. Portsmouth, NH: Heinemann.

Brown, B. (2012). *Daring greatly: How the courage to be vulnerable transforms the way we live, love, parent, and lead*. New York, NY: Gotham Books.

Bryant, J., & Sweet, M. (2014). *The right word: Roget and his thesaurus*. Grand Rapids, MI: Eerdmans Books for Young Readers.

Bunting, E. [Author], & Himler, R. [Illustrator]. (1991). *Fly away home*. New York: Clarion Books.

Calkins, L. M. (2001). *The art of teaching reading*. New York, NY: Addison Wesley.

Cambourne, B. (1995). Toward an educationally relevant theory of literacy learning: Twenty years of inquiry. *The Reading Teacher, 49*(3), 182–190.

Cameron, A. [Author], & Allen, T. [Illustrator]. (1988). *The most beautiful place in the world*. New York, NY: Knopf.

Collins, K. (2008). *Reading for real: Teach students to read with power, intention, and joy in K–3 classrooms*. Portsmouth, NH: Heinemann.

Council of Chief State School Officers & National Governors Association Center for Best Practices. (2010). *Common Core State Standards for English language arts and literacy in history/social studies, science, and technical subjects*. Retrieved from http://www.corestandards.org/ELA-Literacy/

Csikszentmihalyi, M. (1990). *Flow: The psychology of optimal experience*. New York, NY: Harper & Row.

Dashner, J. (2009). *The maze runner*. New York, NY: Delacorte Press.

Deresiewicz, W. (2014). *Excellent sheep: The miseducation of the American elite and the way to a meaningful life*. New York, NY: Free Press.

Duckworth, A. L., Kirby, T., Tsukayama, E., Berstein, H., & Ericsson, K. A. (2010). Deliberate practice spells success: Why grittier competitors triumph at the National Spelling Bee. *Social Psychological and Personality Science, 2*(2), 174–181.

Duckworth, A. L., Peterson, C., Matthews, M. D., & Kelly, D. R. (2007). Grit: Perseverance and passion for long-term goals. *Journal of Personality and Social Psychology, 92*(6), 1087–1101.

Duckworth, A. L., Quinn, P. D., & Seligman, M. E. P. (2009). Positive predictors of teacher effectiveness. *Journal of Positive Psychology, 4*(6), 540–547.

Duckworth Lab. (2015, May 12). *Research statement*. University of Pennsylvania. Retrieved from https://sites.sas.upenn.edu/duckworth/pages/research-statement

Duke, N., & Pearson, P. D. (2001). Effective practices for developing reading comprehension. In A. E. Farstrup & S. J. Samuels (Eds.), *What research has to say about reading instruction* (3rd ed., pp. 205–242). Newark, DE: International Reading Association.

Dweck, C. (2006). *Mindset: The new psychology of success*. New York, NY: Random House.

Dweck, C. (2007). The perils and promise of praise. *Educational Leadership, 65*(2), 34–39. Retrieved from http://www.ascd.org/publications/educational-leadership/oct07/vol65/num02/The-Perils-and-Promises-of-Praise.aspx

Eskreis-Winkler, L., Duckworth, A. L., Shulman, E., & Beale, S. (2014). The grit effect: Predicting retention in the military, the workplace, school and marriage. *Frontiers in Personality Science and Individual Differences, 5*(36), 1–12.

Flores, B., Cousin, P. T., & Diaz, E. (1991). Transforming deficit myths about learning, language, and culture. *Language Arts, 68*, 369–379.

Freire, P. (1970). *Pedagogy of the oppressed*. New York, NY: Continuum.

French, H. W. (2001). *E. O. Wilson's theory of everything*. Retrieved from http://www.theatlantic.com/magazine/archive/2011/11/e-o-wilsons-theory-of-everything/308686/

Godin, S. (2012). *Stop stealing dreams: What is school for?* Retrieved from http://sethgodin.hubpages.com/hub/stop-stealing-dreams

Goldberg, G. (2010). *High school students' experiences in a newly participatory English classroom*. Doctoral dissertation, Teachers College, Columbia University.

Goldberg, G. (2014). *Readers who keep us up at night: Moving away from deficit beliefs and into positive action*. Portsmouth, NH: Heinemann Digital Campus. Retrieved from http://www.heinemann.com/digitalcampus/

Goldberg, G., & Serravallo, J. (2007). *Conferring with readers: Supporting each student's growth and independence*. Portsmouth, NH: Heinemann.

Gray, P. (2013). *Free to learn: Why unleashing the instinct to play will make our children happier, more self-reliant, and better students for life*. New York, NY: Basic Books.

Harvey, S., & Daniels, H. (2009). *Comprehension and collaboration: Inquiry circles in action*. Portsmouth, NH: Heinemann.

Harvey, S., & Goudvis, A. (2007). *Strategies that work: Teaching comprehension for understanding and engagement* (2nd ed.). Portland, ME: Stenhouse.

Hattie, J. (2012). *Visible learning for teachers: Maximizing impact on learning.* London, UK: Routledge.

The Hawn Foundation. (2011). *The MindUP curriculum: Brain-focused strategies for learning—and living.* New York, NY: Scholastic.

Johnston, P. (2004). *Choice words: How our language affects children's learning.* Portland, ME: Stenhouse.

Johnston, P. (2012). *Opening minds: Using language to change lives.* Portland, ME: Stenhouse.

Kehret, P. (2004). *Escaping the giant wave.* New York, NY: Aladdin.

Kindlon, D., & Thompson, M. (2000). *Raising Cain: Protecting the emotional life of boys.* New York, NY: Ballantine Books.

Lepper, M., Greene, D., & Nisbett, R. (1973). Undermining children's intrinsic interest with extrinsic rewards: A test of the overjustification hypothesis. *Journal of Personality and Social Psychology, 28*(1), 129–137.

Meyer, S. (2006). *Twilight.* New York, NY: Little Brown Books.

Miller, D., & Moss, B. (2013). *No more independent reading without support.* Portsmouth, NH: Heinemann.

National Council of Teachers of English. (2009). *Adolescent literacy brief.* Retrieved from www.ncte.org/library/NCTEFiles/Resources/ . . . /AdolLitResearchBrief.pdf

Pearson, P. D. (2011). The roots of reading comprehension instruction. In M. Kamil, P. D. Pearson, E. Moje, & P. Afflerbach (Eds.), *Handbook of reading research* (Vol. 4, Chapter 1). London, UK: Routledge.

Pink, D. (2009). *Drive: The surprising truth about what motivates us.* New York, NY: Riverhead Books.

Rakestraw, M. (2012, June 21). What we see depends on what we look for. *Humane Connection.* Retrieved from http://humaneeducation.org/blog/2012/06/21/what-we-see-depends-on-what-we-look-for/

Reynolds, P. (2004). *Ish.* Cambridge, MA: Candlewick Press.

Robertson-Kraft, C., & Duckworth, A. L. (2014). True grit: Trait-level perseverance and passion for long-term goals predicts effectiveness and retention among novice teachers. *Teachers College Record, 116*(3), 1–27.

Robinson, K., & Aronica, L. (2009). *The element: How finding your passion changes everything.* New York, NY: Viking.

Rock, D. (2006). *Quiet leadership: Help people think better—don't tell them what to do: Six steps to transforming performance at work.* New York, NY: Collins.

Saltzberg, B. (2010). *Beautiful oops!* New York: Workman.

Skinner, E. A., Zimmer-Gembeck, M. J., & Connell, J. P. (1998). Individual differences and the development of perceived control. *Monographs of the Society for Research in Child Development, 254*(63), 2–3.

Snow, C., & O'Connor, C. (2013). *Close reading and far-reaching classroom discussion: Fostering a vital connection* [A policy brief from the Literacy Research Panel of the International Reading Association]. Retrieved from http://www.reading.org/Libraries/lrp/ira-lrp-policy-brief--close-reading--13sept2013.pdf

Spires, A. (2014). *The most magnificent thing*. New York, NY: Kids Can Press.

Stewart, M. (2014). *How is my brain like a supercomputer?* New York, NY: Sterling.

Tough, P. (2013). *How children succeed: Grit, curiosity, and the hidden power of character*. New York, NY: Mariner Books.

Weeks, S. (2011). *As simple as it gets*. New York, NY: HarperCollins.

Willems, M. (2009). *Naked mole rat gets dressed*. New York, NY: Hyperion Books for Children.

Woodson, J. [Author], & Lewis, E. [Illustrator]. (2001). *The other side*. New York, NY: Putnam.

Index

Achor, S., 41, 54, 182, 186
Active listening, 96–98, 99, 110
Active literacy, 8, 9, 17
Admiring lens, 2–3, 34, 39–40
  big/small pictures, focus on, 50–52
  deficit thinking and, 40–41, 45, 56,
    121, 196, 199
  growth mindset, support of, 52–55
  guiding questions for, 56–57
  individuality, recognition/
    appreciation of, 47–48
  language choices, student mindset
    and, 55
  listening, art of, 98
  meaning-making process,
    discussion about, 45
  mentor role, trouble with, 168–171
  miner role, trouble with, 111–113
  mirror role, trouble with, 130–133
  model role, trouble with, 149–152
  potential, recognition/appreciation
    of, 45–46
  precision, pursuit of, 48–50
  Pygmalion Effect and, 55
  seeing what's there and, 40–42
  student thinking, access to, 43–45
  trust and, 196
  See also Admiring lens strategies;
    Curiosity-based approach;
    Teacher roles; Teaching process
Admiring lens strategies, 173–175
  feedback, listen/look/label strategy
    and, 188
  feedback, outcome analysis/
    discussion and, 189
  feedback strategies and, 187–189
  goal creation from categories
    and, 181
  goal setting strategies and, 179–182
  goals, class list of, 180
  goals, personalization of, 182

growth mindset, development of,
    186–187
  mindset analysis, characters'
    mindsets and, 184
  mindset analysis, readers' mindsets
    and, 185
  mindset lessons, read alouds
    and, 183
  mindset reflections and, 182–187
  reading process, description of, 176
  reading process, focus on, 175–179
  reading process terminology
    and, 179
  reading process, visual
    representations of, 177–178
  support needs, clarity in, 190
  support, sources of, 191
  support strategies and, 189–191
  See also Admiring lens;
    Curiosity-based approach
Agency, 33–36
Allington, R., 7
Anderson, C., 126
Aronica, L., 45
Assigner role, 8–9, 11, 12, 34,
    138–139
Authentic learning, 9–10, 11
  gradual release model of
    instruction and, 33–36
  play and, 18, 21
  See also Motivation; Ownership;
    Reader-ownership classrooms

Balanced literacy model, 7, 33, 206
Barnhouse, D., 45
Beale, S., 25
Blau, S., 14, 15, 54
Brain function:
  adrenaline and, 24
  amygdala and, 106
  dopamine and, 24

eureka moments and, 24
hippocampus and, 106
optimal performance zones and, 24, 106
prefrontal cortex and, 106
problem-solving process and, 24
serotonin and, 24
teacher intervention, impediment of, 24, 106
threats, response to, 106
Brown, B., 117, 118, 120, 122, 123, 125, 195, 196, 203
Bryant, J., 50
Bunting, E., 166

Calkins, L. M., 39
Cambourne, B., 136
Cameron, A., 163
Collins, K., 148
Common Core State Standards (CCSS), 93, 94
Compliance, 2, 8, 16, 17, 27, 29, 205
Csikszentmihalyi, M., 24
Curiosity-based approach, 40, 195
    admiring lens and, 56, 196
    balanced literacy model and, 206
    classroom physical space, changes in, 200–201
    collegial feedback, shift toward, 202–203
    deficit lens-to-admiring lens shift and, 199
    mentor role and, 198
    miner role and, 114, 197
    mirror role and, 198
    model role and, 198
    reader ownership, shift toward, 205
    readers, observation of, 56, 94–95
    Student-Focused Reading Checklist and, 199, 204
    student-led feedback, shift toward, 202
    teacher focus-to-student focus shift and, 199–200

teacher roles, progression through, 197–199
teacher self-admiring beliefs and, 203
vulnerability, trust development and, 195–196, 203
See also Admiring lens; Teacher roles

Daniels, S., 15
Dashner, J., 94
Deficit lens, 34, 40, 45, 56, 121, 196, 199
Duckworth, A. L., 25, 54
Duke, N. K., 14
Dweck, C., 52, 53, 122, 182

Eskreis-Winkler, L., 25
Eureka moment, 24

Feedback:
    process-oriented feedback and, 55
    rarity of, 117–118
    Reading Workshop model and, 4, 20, 33
    See also Admiring lens strategies; Curiosity-based approach; Mirror role
Fixed mindset, 53, 54, 55, 81, 109, 123

Globalization pressures, 17
Goldberg, G., 16, 204, 205, 206, 207, 209, 211, 213
Gradual release model of instruction, 33–36
Gray, P., 21
Greene, D., 18
Grit, 24–26, 54
Growth mindset, 10, 23, 25, 27–28
    admiring lens and, 52–55
    challenge, acceptance of, 53, 54
    deliberate practice, opportunities for, 54
    expectations of, 54–55

fixed mindset and, 53, 54, 55, 81,
    109, 123
grit and, 54
highly literate readers and, 54
language choices, impacts of, 55
mindset types chart and, 81, 83
Pygmalion Effect and, 55
reader mindset, uncovering
    of, 109
See also Admiring lens strategies;
    Curiosity-based approach;
    Mentor role; Mirror role;
    Ownership; Reader-ownership
    classrooms

Harvey, S., 8, 15
Hattie, J., 2, 25, 26, 40, 43, 54

Independent reading, 1, 3
active literacy and, 8, 9
authentic learning and, 9–10
classroom environment and,
    13, 17
comprehension, factors in, 14
individualization and, 13
intrinsic motivation and, 18,
    20–21
performative literacy and, 14–15
reader-focused classrooms and,
    11–14, 17
Reading Workshop model and, 4–8
student engagement and, 13,
    15–16
Student-Focused Reading Checklist
    and, 13, 14, 100, 204
transfer and, 13, 14, 16, 124–126
See also Curiosity-based approach;
    Growth mindset; Motivation;
    Ownership; Reader-ownership
    classrooms; Self-directed
    reading; Student achievement;
    Teacher roles
International Literacy Association, 93
Intrinsic motivation, 18, 20–21

Johnston, P., 10, 33, 34, 55, 119, 123

Kehret, P., 144
Kelly, D. R., 25
Kindlon, D., 24

Lepper, M., 18
Levitt, T., 29
Lightbulb moments, 24
Literacy. *See* Balanced literacy model;
    Independent reading; Miner role;
    Reader-ownership classrooms;
    Reading Workshop model

Manager role, 9, 11, 12, 34
Matthews, M. D., 25
Mentor role, 28, 29–30, 31, 155–156
action steps, focus on, 159–160
mentoring process and, 156–157
one-step-at-a-time approach and,
    157–158
prompts, clarity in, 159, 160–161
reproducible chart for, 213
small group mentoring and,
    162–166
strategies, defined steps in, 157
support, gradual withdrawal of,
    161–162
telling vs. questioning, comparison
    of, 158–159
trouble with, resolution of,
    168–171
whole class mentoring and,
    166–168
See also Curiosity-based approach;
    Teacher roles
Miller, D., 45
Mindset. *See* Admiring lens;
    Admiring lens strategies;
    Curiosity-based approach; Fixed
    mindset; Growth mindset
Miner role, 30, 31, 91–92
class reading process, observation
    of, 107–109
Common Core State Standards
    and, 94
data collection/documentation
    and, 98–100, 101, 102

five-step process in, 92–100, 106, 108–109, 114

formative assessment and, 93, 104–105

growth vs. fixed mindset responses and, 109

individual reading process, observation of, 99, 100–105

listening, art of, 96–98, 99, 110

mining purpose, determination of, 93–94, 97

observing the reader and, 94–95, 97, 99

process-oriented questioning and, 96, 97, 99, 103–104, 108

reader-centered conversations and, 105–106

reader mindset, uncovering of, 109

reproducible chart for, 207

role utilization, timing of, 110–111

teacher-centered quizzes and, 105, 106

trends, emergence of, 100

trouble with, resolution of, 111–113

See also Curiosity-based approach; Teacher roles

Mirror role, 30, 31, 117

asset-based feedback and, 119, 121–122

deficit lens and, 121

feedback, student learning/engagement and, 117–118

five qualities of feedback and, 119, 120–126

growth mindset feedback, usefulness of, 118, 119, 122–123, 126

nonjudgmental feedback and, 119, 125–126

preparation for, 119–120

process-focused feedback and, 119, 122–123, 124

reproducible chart for, 209

small group feedback and, 126–128

specific feedback and, 118, 119, 120–121, 124

teaching function of feedback and, 119

transferrable feedback and, 119, 124–125

trouble with, resolution of, 130–133

whole class feedback and, 129–130

See also Curiosity-based approach; Teacher roles

Model role, 10, 31, 33, 135

assigner role, avoidance of, 148–149

cross-text strategies and, 139

demonstration of strategies and, 137–141, 144–145, 146

explaining strategies used and, 137, 144, 146

individual student, modeling for, 143–146

modeling process, actions in, 137–142, 146

naming/summarizing action and, 142, 145, 146

optimal literacy learning, conditions for, 136

preparation for, 148

previewing/monitoring strategies and, 139

reproducible chart for, 211

support, gradual withdrawal of, 161–162

teaching/learning process and, 135–136

text-specific strategies and, 139

trouble with, resolution of, 149–152

whole class, modeling for, 147–148

See also Curiosity-based approach; Teacher role

Monitor role, 9, 11, 12, 34

Moss, B., 45

Motivation:

carrot-and-stick structure of, 18

deficit lens and, 41

fixed mindset and, 53, 54, 55
grit, impact of, 24–26
instructional practices, motivation
    challenges and, 18–21
intrinsic motivation and, 18,
    20–21
optimal performance zones and, 24
play, deep understanding and,
    18, 21
problem-solving process and, 24
reader-owned classrooms and,
    15–16, 29
reading conference checklists
    and, 20
reading log entries and, 19–20
reading notebook entries and, 19
reward systems and, 18, 20–21
Sawyer Effect and, 18
struggle, value of, 23–26
See also Admiring lens strategies;
    Growth mindset; Independent
    reading; Ownership; Reader-
    ownership classrooms; Self-
    directed reading; Student
    achievement; Teacher roles

National Council of Teachers of
    English, 11
Nisbett, R., 18

O'Connor, C., 93
Ownership, 14
    balanced literacy model,
        continuum of responsibility
        and, 33
    choice, exercise of, 15, 17, 21, 30
    compliance vs. reader-owned
        classrooms and, 16, 17
    comprehension, factors in,
        14, 15
    crisis in, 16
    facets of, 15
    globalization pressures and, 17
    gradual release model of
        instruction and, 33–36
    grit, impact of, 24–26

instructional practices, shift in,
    26–30, 205
intrinsic motivation and, 18,
    20–21
performative literacy and,
    14–15
problem solving, brain mapping
    function and, 24
rigor and, 17
self-directed reading and, 15, 21
struggle, value of, 23–26
student engagement/motivation
    and, 15–16, 26
student roles and, 31–32
teacher-student relationship
    continuum and, 27
transfer and, 16
See also Independent reading;
    Motivation; Reader-ownership
    classrooms; Self-directed
    reading; Teacher roles;
    Teaching process

Pearson, P. D., 14
Performative literacy, 14–15
Peterson, C., 25
Pink, D., 18
Play, 18, 21
Problem-solving process, 24
Pygmalion Effect, 55

Quinn, P. D., 25

Rakestraw, M., 56
Reader-ownership classrooms, 59
    book club tools/spaces and,
        73, 74, 80
    class goals chart and, 71
    class meeting area and, 63–64
    digital reading notebooks and, 67
    independent thought charts
        and, 79
    individual student intentions
        charting and, 74
    library area and, 64
    mindset types chart and, 81, 83

reading classroom space spiral and, 61

reading nooks/personal space and, 76–78

reading notebooks and, 65–69, 80, 86–88

reading process spiral and, 60

reading volume tracking charts and, 70

Reading Workshop space and, 62

research topics list and, 72

small group instruction and, 75

student-organized notebooks and, 80

student reflections and, 82, 83–85

writing choice charts and, 68–69

See also Admiring lens strategies; Independent reading; Mentor role; Miner role; Mirror role; Model role; Ownership; Self-directed reading

Reading classroom space spiral, 61

Reading process spiral, 50, 177

See also Admiring lens strategies; Independent reading; Miner role; Self-directed reading

Reading Workshop model, 4

classroom physical space and, 61, 62

conferencing/feedback and, 4, 20, 33

elements in, 4

independent reading and, 4, 5, 33

minilessons and, 4–5

motivation structures and, 18–20

partnerships/teaching share and, 4, 7–8

process of, 4–7

reading log entries and, 19–20

reading notebooks and, 19, 65–69

workshop structures checklist and, 4, 7, 8

See also Balanced literacy model; Independent reading; Reader-ownership classrooms; Teaching process

Reinforcement. *See* Motivation

Reward systems, 18, 20–21

Reynolds, P. H., 183

Rigor, 17

Robertson-Kraft, C., 25

Robinson, K., 45

Rock, D., 24

Roget, P., 48, 50

Roles. *See* Curiosity-based approach; Mentor role; Miner role; Mirror role; Model role; Teacher roles

Saleebey, D., 122

Saltzberg, B., 183

Sawyer Effect, 18

Self-directed reading, 15

compliance and, 16, 17

grit, impact of, 24–26

intrinsic motivation and, 18, 20–21

reader-owned classrooms and, 17, 29–30

See also Admiring lens strategies; Independent reading; Motivation; Ownership; Reader-ownership classrooms

Seligman, M. E. P., 25

Shulman, E., 25

Snow, C., 93

Standardized tests, 25

STEAM (science/technology/ engineering/arts/math) curriculum, 39–40

STEM (science/technology/ engineering/math) curriculum, 39

Student achievement:

active literacy and, 8, 9, 17

agency, development of, 33–36

authentic learning and, 9–10, 11

basic principles for, 3

compliance vs. learning and, 2, 8, 16, 17

globalization pressures and, 17

grit, impact of, 24–26

instructional practices and, 2

intrinsic motivation and, 18, 20–21
struggle, value of, 23–26
transfer and, 13, 14, 16
See also Admiring lens strategies; Curiosity-based approach; Growth mindset; Independent reading; Motivation; Ownership; Reader-ownership classrooms; Teacher roles
Student-Focused Reading Checklist, 13, 14, 100, 204
Sweet, M., 50

Take-charge independence. *See* Independent reading; Ownership; Reader-ownership classrooms; Self-directed reading
Teacher roles, 8
assigner role and, 8–9, 11, 12, 34, 138–139
balanced literacy model, continuum of responsibility and, 33, 206
compliance and, 2, 8, 16, 17, 27, 29, 205
demonstrations and, 35–36
gradual release model and, 33–36
grit, impact of, 24–26
growth mindset and, 23, 27–28
guided practice and, 35–36
helpfulness, epidemic of, 23–26
language use and, 10
manager role and, 9, 11, 12, 34
mentor role and, 28, 29–30, 31
miner role, 30, 31
mirror role, 30, 31
model role, 10, 31, 33
monitor role, 9, 11, 12, 34
optimal performance zones and, 24
problem-solving process and, 24
productive talk, power of, 10, 28–29

reader ownership, shift towards, 26–36
student ownership roles and, 31–32, 35–36
student struggle, value of, 23–26
student thought process, access to, 28–29, 92
teacher-student relationship continuum and, 27, 34
See also Admiring lens; Curiosity-based approach; Mentor role; Miner role; Mirror role; Model role; Teaching process
Teaching process, 1–2
active literacy and, 8, 9, 17
admiring lens and, 2–3, 34, 39–40
compliance vs. learning and, 2, 8, 16, 17, 27
deficit lens and, 34, 40, 45, 56, 121, 196, 199
reader-focused instruction and, 11–14, 17
Reading Workshop model and, 4–8, 18
research findings and, 2, 3
student private world, accessibility of, 2, 28–29
traditional approach to, 7
See also Admiring lens; Admiring lens strategies; Curiosity-based approach; Motivation; Ownership; Reader-ownership classrooms; Teacher roles
Thompson, M., 24
Tough, P., 24
Transfer, 13, 14, 16, 124–126
Trust, 195–196, 203

Vinton, V., 45

Weeks, S., 27
Wilson, E. O., 50, 51
Woodson, J., 166

A SAGE Company

Helping educators make the greatest impact

CORWIN HAS ONE MISSION: to enhance education through intentional professional learning.

We build long-term relationships with our authors, educators, clients, and associations who partner with us to develop and continuously improve the best evidence-based practices that establish and support lifelong learning.

CL CORWIN LITERACY

Doug Fisher & Nancy Frey

On how text-dependent questions can inspire close and critical thinking

Sara Holbrook & Michael Salinger

On how to teach today's i-touch generation precision writing and reading in any subject

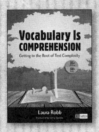

Laura Robb

On helping students tackle the biggest barrier of complex texts

Gretchen Bernabei

On 101 lessons to help students master the conventions of grammar and usage once and for all

Nancy Akhavan

On top-notch nonfiction lessons and texts for maximizing students' content area comprehension

Corwin educator discount

20% off
every day

To order your copies, visit **www.corwin.com/literacy**

BECAUSE ALL TEACHERS ARE LEADERS

Also Available

Sharon Taberski & Leslie Blauman

On what the grades K–2 and 3–5 standards really say, really mean, and how to put them into practice

Janiel Wagstaff & Leslie Blauman

On 50+ reading and writing lessons to boost your instructional potency

Jim Burke

On what the 6–8 and 9–12 standards really say, really mean, and how to put them into practice

Nancy Frey & Doug Fisher

On 5 Access Points for seriously stretching students' capacity to comprehend complex text

Nancy Boyles

On the whys and hows of getting close reading right in grades 3–6

Nancy Boyles

On ready-to-go units and planning tools to ramp up close reading

CL CORWIN LITERACY

N15887

31901056834999